The DUH! Book
of
Management and Supervision

Dispelling Common Leadership Myths

*A Practical Guide For Leaders
That Reminds Us Of The Obvious*

Gerri King, Ph.D.

"DUH!"

pronounced DUH but prolonging the UUUH,
pitching the voice a bit low, and inflecting it with an intonation
of incredulousness or sarcasm or both.

Formal definition of DUH: "Of course"

Informal or slang definition of DUH:
a sarcastic response used when someone states the obvious.

The DUH! Book of Management and Supervision: Dispelling Common Leadership Myths

Printed in the United States of America

First Printing 2014

ISBN: 978-0-9661878-4-7

Publisher	**Common Sense Press** 85 Warren Street Concord, NH 03301
Cover Design	Lewis Agrell
Book Design	Ron King
Ordering	Special discounts are available on quantity purchases by corporations, associations, and others. For details contact the publisher at the address above or email gerri@gerriking.com
	Orders by U.S. trade bookstores and wholesalers. Please contact the publisher at the address above.

Dedicated to

My husband Ron and our son Ethan
who are intuitively fair and hire people they respect
resulting in the Natural Playgrounds Company
striving to become a model organization.

and

To my clients who do so much right.

Contents

Acknowledgments

I am so appreciative of the inspiration and help I received.

Thanks to

My husband Ron, whose talent still has me in awe, for using the time he doesn't have to help edit, format, and support me. I am ever grateful.

Our son, Ethan, who since the age of 5, has carried the mantel of the most fascinating person I know. As a business leader, and because of who he is, he will no doubt debate some of the points I make. It will be a dress rehearsal for others who are bound to challenge me.

My parents who, when they were alive, balanced out any insecurities I had with often unrealistic and loving faith in me.

Extended family and friends who have heard about this book for so long, they probably thought it was published years ago.

Colleagues, both at HDA and with whom I've partnered, for providing inspiration, balance, and counterpoint.

My adored Book Club who will be kind enough not to throw this book across the room, even in honor of our dear departed Laura.

The Fab 5 with whom I have met once a year since we finished our Ph.D.s and with whom I wish I could meet twice a day.

The Fab 4 who were my best friends in adolescence and remain so important to me. I treasure you.

And finally, to my clients and audiences with whom I've shared these insights. Thank you for taking me seriously while laughing. I'm grateful.

Introduction

I spend my professional life consulting, training, and facilitating in both the public and private sectors, and have become aware of how desperate many managers and supervisors are for help.

The stories that follow are from my own experience and those of other professionals who have shared familiar tales. Their consistency is both comforting and unnerving, the former because it's the norm and the latter because - well - it's the norm.

Most people are promoted to supervisory and leadership positions because they're good at their jobs, but being good at one's profession is a very different job from supervising or leading employees.

This brings me to the reason I wrote the book.

After years of observation, I can say with certainty that many common management practices aren't effective. It is why I call them "Myths" and why I question traditional wisdom. I offer opinions with which you may not agree. If so, you have a lot of company.

I feel free to tell you what I believe without apology because I trust you'll adopt only what rings true for you. Accept what makes sense, throw out what doesn't, and put on the shelf what you may want to take down some day.

If it appears simplistic, I've done my job because neglecting the obvious is often the reason that problems arise.

One final note: if the Myths look like Facts to you, I'm sorry. You're probably annoyed that you bought the book.

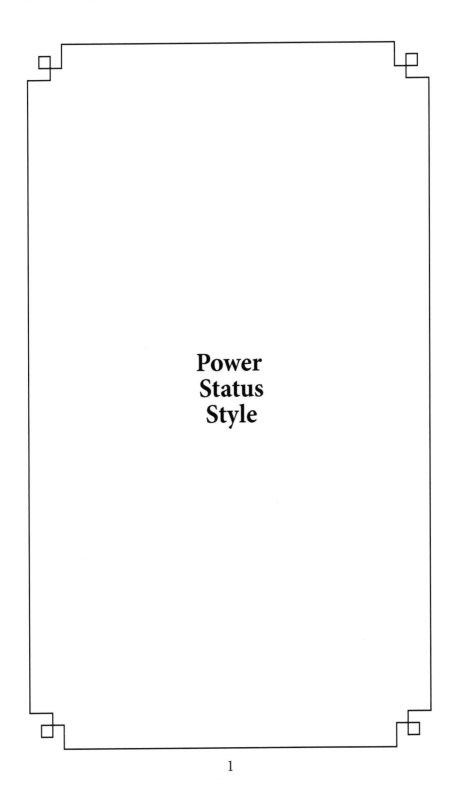

**Power
Status
Style**

myth

Top Management must present a united front

If you value honesty and diversity, do you want to lie to your employees and pretend that you are all in agreement when you're not?

Why not tell them that coming to certain conclusions was difficult and consider sharing the points of disagreement and how you finally arrived at consensus?

It's fine to say that you're united in the final decision and implementation, but the staff will feel much better knowing that their concerns were considered, that it was not an easy road, and that you painstakingly arrived at consensus after thoughtful discourse.

Story

One enlightened leadership team decided to tell the truth. They would announce decisions and agreements and then tell everyone how they got there. They often shared that it was not easy and that – at least at the outset – there was widespread disagreement. They described the various opinions and how they finally came to conclusions. They even talked about lingering concerns and asked the staff for help in resolving the remaining issues.

As a result, the employees felt included and not infantilized. Their willingness to "sign on" was unprecedented. They reported that it was empowering to be trusted with the truth.

myth

Titles ensure power

Not really. Power is the ability to influence and requires the implicit consent of others. If they don't give it to you, your title could be meaningless.

Story

We need only to look at recent world history for examples of rulers dethroned when they were no longer supported by their people. Apartheid years ago and the more recent Arab Spring are just two examples.

Though on a much smaller scale, organizational leaders are similarly vulnerable. Just because people at the top possess titles and are seemingly secure in their positions, it does not mean that they have the support of their employees. Without it, influence is not sustainable because the person in charge risks not receiving necessary information or the loyalty that success requires.

myth

It's the title that should be respected

Status may describe your position, but not your competence, which has to be proven over time.

Once accomplished, it's acceptable to be self-confident, but there's no justification for treating others as though they're not as worthy.

Story

An airline had to cancel a flight, which is always a difficult scenario. Cutting the rebooking line, a gentleman slapped his ticket on the counter and yelled, "I need to be on the next flight, first class!" "Sir, I have a long line here and I need you to get in it and wait your turn," said the agent. Furious, he asked, "Do you know who I am?"

Frustrated, and at the end of her patience, she got on the public address system and said, "There's a man at my counter who doesn't know who he is. Can someone help him?"

I'm not advocating revenge but have to admit that this brings a smile.

myth

If you believe in shared power it's easy to make the transition

Keep in mind that shared power is based on expertise not role, and knowledge not position. There are several reasons people are afraid to give up control: they feel they can do it better themselves; if they give power to others, things might get screwed up; or they may be giving up something that fuels their confidence.

When you share power, you're trusting others to make informed decisions, but the move from a hierarchical to a self-directed organization does have challenges.

Story

The founding President of the company decided that sharing power would result in a more responsive organization, so he initiated a program that trained employees to make decisions at their levels of expertise. It worked beautifully until a woman mistakenly sent out a huge check to an undeserving client who cashed it.

The President called everyone together. People were nervous and apprehensive because they thought he was going to make a public example of her before she was fired.

He looked at her and said, "If it had been a $5.00 check, we would have said, 'Apparently, we didn't train you well enough,' but this check was for an enormous amount of money!"

Nervous silence followed, but then he looked at her and said, "Apparently, we didn't train you well enough."

That was it. She went back to work and everyone vowed to assess what went wrong and how it could be prevented from happening again.

myth

Credentials should dictate salary

Higher education promises success, the likelihood of promotions, and increased salary, but there are some progressive employers who question the practice. It's a hard sell because it goes against our pervasive system of compensation.

Story

The owner/president of a company began very modestly. It was just him and an administrative assistant. They grew to be almost 200 strong and the model they followed was not unusual: hiring professional people and paying them based on whether they had a bachelor's, master's, or doctoral degree.

One day the owner realized that his able administrative assistant, now office manager, could only afford to send her children to college if she left her job and got a degree so she could make more money. She was responsible for much of the company's success and it was clear that without her, they would not be where they were.

He decided that she should be compensated based on criteria within her job description and how well she performed. She now makes more than most people with graduate degrees and in her words "will be loyal for life."

myth

Human Resources does not need to be part of the leadership team

If you're a big enough organization to have a Human Resources Department, then you probably have concerns about a myriad of legal and ethical issues as well as employee morale and workplace concerns. Decisions made in the absence of HR's counsel risk leading to poor results.

Story

The Executive Group traditionally did not include HR which was okay when they just handled benefits. Now HR has become a strategic partner in advocating for employees and the well-being of the organization. They have responsibility for employee welfare and are rightly seen as the legal and moral conscience of the company.

After just a few meetings that included the HR Director, the President observed that she provided more counsel and information than anyone else on the management team. Within months it became clear that she deserved a permanent seat at the table.

The group knew they had made the right decision when they found themselves regularly saying, "Thank goodness you're here!"

myth

The best mentors are supervisors

How safe is it to tell one's supervisor about professional struggles and doubts? The mentoring environment should provide a secure and protected experience in which an employee can learn through trial and error. For that reason, though supervisors do engage in mentoring, a formal mentor should not contribute to the employee's performance evaluation, nor should s/he be expected to report to anyone about the employee's progress or challenges.

Think about mentors as providing "shortcut vehicles." They share knowledge, experience, and mistakes that would be hard for the person to discover on her or his own. In that spirit, employees learn from their mentor's failures as well as their successes. "A mentor provides the wisdom of a lifetime, minus the pain of acquiring it." (Author unknown, but it's a perfect description.)

Story

A corporation decided to set up a mentoring program they defined as an alliance between senior and junior members of the company. The program was clearly outlined, as were boundaries, expectations, training, and shared meaning about how it would work and the benefits that would result.

To their delight, the design served both the company and employees well. It allowed for faster assimilation and the sharpening of skills, as well as easier transitioning to new positions. Most importantly, the company became known as a mentoring organization delivering the message that their success was a reflection of the progress of their people.

It's become a premier learning environment.

myth

Saying you have an Open Door Policy is all you need to appear welcoming

We forget that "open door" is a metaphor. Some supervisors with wide-open office doors deliver the message that they're always too busy to talk, while others who work behind closed doors are infinitely interruptible.

Story

One CEO realized that her employees didn't believe her open door policy. This was a problem, because she wanted the interaction but didn't know how to encourage it.

Furthermore, she couldn't stand sitting around waiting for someone to come through the door, so she kept herself busy, which meant that whenever an employee did venture in, it was definitely an interruption.

She decided to put up a sign that said "From 10:30 - 11:30 AM, I welcome your interruptions, or at any other time if it's urgent or especially important."

It worked out great. Instead of dribbling in all day, people were usually fine waiting until the next morning, and since she had the hour scheduled into her calendar, she didn't resent the diversion.

myth

The supervisor's job
is to make people productive

No, the supervisor's job is to create an environment where people can be productive. There is a difference.

Creating an atmosphere of safety and support allows and encourages a constructive work place. Looming over people only encourages dependence and blind obedience, which is risky because employee suggestions for improvement may not be forthcoming and essential knowledge may be withheld.

Story

This particular supervisor had risen through the ranks and was able to perform every job in her department. That prompted her to take over when things weren't going well. Predictably, independent motivation diminished and her employees waited for her to tell them what to do.

It worked for awhile but, as time went on, she was increasingly out of the day-to-day loop and not as up on the nuances of the various tasks. Those who worked for her learned to defer and their creativity and ingenuity steadily declined, as did the quality of their work.

Both internal and external customers began to notice, yet the supervisor still thought she was more qualified than others in the department. It wasn't until a trusted colleague said, "You're making the same mistake I made and it's taken a year for my department to recover. Now that I'm not the 'beginning and end all,' we're finally meeting the standard I thought only I could reach."

myth

Employees feel comfortable bringing problems to the boss

Too many employees keep secrets from their supervisors because those in charge have a dual role: to help with problems and to evaluate performance. When supervisees worry that their inadequacies might show up on their evaluations, they may choose to keep problems to themselves.

That's what fear does. It gets in the way of reasonable dialogue and inquiry and discourages owning up to mistakes and taking responsibility. "I'd rather you tell me the truth, than keep silent," we teach our children, yet the same standard doesn't always apply to adults.

Story

The top administration shared their frustration about the guys on the manufacturing floor not bringing problems to the forefront until it was too late. Had they owned up earlier, they could have been easily resolved. By the time the foremen heard about them, their severity had increased and options for solutions had narrowed.

When they sat down to have an honest dialogue, a few brave people told them why. "If we come to you with the same issue more than once, you're going to think we're incompetent and it's going to be reflected in our evaluations. It's just too chancy."

They all vowed to change that dynamic. It wasn't easy, but after a few tries, everyone began to slowly trust that it was more rewarding to bring concerns forward early on than to wait. One man observed, "We're not there yet, but we're also not as intimidated as we used to be."

myth

Your way is the best way

For you, perhaps, but is it important that they do it your way or is it important that they get it done? Sometimes protocol and procedures require things to be done a specific way, but too often we're tempted to insist on a process because we can't easily imagine another approach.

Story

A veteran section head was dogmatic about how things should be accomplished. Not only was he insistent, he didn't want to hear about any alternatives.

One day his boss challenged him and implied that he was rigid. He agreed and said, "I'm rigid, but I'm also right!" Following a friend's suggestion, he started adding "for me" after "right" and began opening the door to alternatives.

He explained to his employees that he couldn't stop sharing his opinion, but would be adding "for me" after each directive where there was flexibility.

He describes a transformation, both personally and professionally. Now they mostly follow his lead because he has a lot of experience. When they choose to act otherwise, he fakes hitting his head against the wall and walks away laughing. It hasn't been easy, and he often reverts to old habits, but his employees appreciate that he's trying.

myth

The best way to delegate
is to assign tasks to others

That's the proper definition, but merely telling people what to do – and sometimes how to do it – is not the most effective way to share responsibility or build a team.

Story

The supervisor was extremely stressed and his boss encouraged him to delegate rather than take on everything himself, so he did.

He listed the tasks, wrote names beside them, and started handing out duties. He was thoughtful about it, making sure that everything employees were asked to do fell within their skill sets. Nevertheless, people became incredibly disgruntled and felt put upon.

With the help of a facilitator, the staff aired their concerns. To a person, they said that they wished they'd been consulted. They agreed that their supervisor was doing way too much and needed help, and that they should all take on more, but they had trouble with how the work was disseminated.

They asked him why he didn't simply bring the list and allow them to divvy up what had to be done. "We're smart enough to know what we do best! We're not children, after all. You can trust us!"

He produced the list and they all discussed the best way to divide the tasks. For the most part, people happily volunteered. What was left were the duties that no one really wanted, but there were just a few and they were willing to each take a less appealing job. Interestingly, the final iteration was not that different from the one he had originally devised, but now it was their choice.

myth

The boss should oversee all things

There are good reasons that micromanaging has been given a bad rap. It originally meant paying attention to small details but now describes a style where supervisors don't trust their staff, feel that they have to check and control every aspect of their work, and are reluctant to delegate.

The job of the supervisor is to set parameters within which people can exert autonomy. If trained well, they can work without someone looking over their shoulders. If they can't, you should ask yourself why you hired them or what's wrong with the training you're providing.

Story

At a small company where the receptionist was not at his desk during lunch, the supervisor asked different employees to answer the phone for that hour. The response was swift and not good. Accusations that he was playing favorites and not being sensitive to personal needs were daily discussion topics.

I asked him if he really cared who covered for the receptionist on any given day. If he just wanted someone with competence, knowledge, and good customer service skills, why not let the group decide who answers the phone as long as the parameters are met?

With staff help, he issued guidelines and then left the scheduling to them. It proved to be much easier and the kindness they showed one another was evident. If someone could not take a shift, they gladly filled in because the request wasn't coming from a parental-type figure.

myth

Employees should do what the boss says because the boss said it

What if the person in charge is wrong and why go it alone? Wouldn't s/he like some help in monitoring mistakes? Being near the top is lonely enough without creating an autocratic barrier that leads to isolation.

Rank not withstanding, the people with the information should be encouraged to come forth. They must be assured that it's safe to speak up and then issued an invitation. When it's appropriate, they should be effusively thanked for saving your ___!

Story

There are many stories that illustrate this point, but consider the more serious mistakes that are made when people aren't encouraged to challenge authority: the exhausted physician issues the wrong med order; the CEO is missing pivotal information before making a crucial decision; the high ranking political figure risks her or his security because the staff just follows orders; or the Army private observes a potential threat on the front line that the commanding officer hasn't seen.

Even less serious scenarios can have disastrous results.

myth

The best way to be in control of a situation is to exert firm control over others

Trying to exert control by keeping employees under your thumb exhibits insecurity and distrust and may be destructive. Finding a way to understand what's going on and remaining calm and in control of yourself so you feel confident about what you're doing works much better than trying to control the behaviors and activities of others.

Story

An elementary school teacher once told me that when she was feeling out of control, she'd become more controlling and dictatorial. Her students intuitively knew she was not her usual, confident self and it scared them, which made their behavior worse, prompting her to become even more controlling. It was a downward spiral.

She finally learned to go out in the hall, take some deep breaths, and gather strength internally. When she returned to the room in better shape, the kids would calm down.

I contend that adults react similarly, so pay attention to the kids. They are the graduate school of life.

myth

Authoritarian personalities
want to be surrounded by compliant people

On the contrary, people with authoritarian styles prefer like-minded colleagues because it reinforces their autocratic approach. To see others do it differently is inherently threatening and often confusing.

Story

A dictatorial middle manager was taken aback by his new boss's style. The man was gentle, receptive to input, and seemingly lenient. He described himself as a democratic leader who preferred a flat, rather than hierarchical, department.

"Middle Manager Man" was confused and upset when his superior said, "I want you to be autonomous and make your own decisions. If you get stuck, come to me for ideas, but I trust that you have the knowledge and training to decide."

Though this scenario may sound like a dream come true for someone who likes to be in control, it wasn't for him. He couldn't justify his authoritarian approach in such an equitable environment so he left in search of an organization that mirrored his self-described rigidity.

myth

Meetings should be called and led by the person in charge

Do your staff meetings take place if the boss isn't there? Do they take place if the administrative assistant isn't there? The answers are usually "no" to the first, and "yes" to the second.

This implies that people don't have anything to say to each other if the leader isn't present. It also gives a clear message that a person's value in the organization depends on status, meaning that the information and knowledge people have to share is directly related to their importance.

Story

Like children excited about a snow day, everyone at this company looked forward to cancelled meetings, so the transition to hold staff meetings even when supervisors were missing was not happily accepted by leadership or the rest of the employees.

However, they decided to try it anyway and learned that as much, and sometimes more, was accomplished when supervisors were missing, which should not have been a surprise, because the rank and file often provided some of the most important information and had much to contribute.

They began taking better minutes and decided to distribute them so those who were absent were kept up to speed, which was also an improvement.

Employees reported that their confidence was elevated because their input was recognized and acknowledged.

myth

Supervisors have the same leeway as everyone else

Sorry, but as a supervisor, you're not one of the gang. What you do, say, or feel affects many people.

Employees are often too intimidated to check out what's going on with the boss, and because body language is often all they have to go on, there is a chance you'll be misinterpreted or misunderstood. Further, you have no way of seeing your own body language, so you may have no idea what message you're sending.

It's not unusual to hear about employees "walking on eggs" for 3 days because their supervisor looked unhappy, even though the reason for the unhappiness might be completely disconnected from the workplace.

At the very least, the boss should say, "It's not about you or about here," while also creating an atmosphere where supervisees feel comfortable asking if they have anything to do with your state of mind.

Story

Imagine you have a flat tire and come into work looking crabby. If the staff doesn't know that you're in a bad mood because of your ordeal, they'll think it's because of something they did. When you tell them the reason you're upset, they're thrilled. They don't care if you're grouchy. They just care if they're responsible for it.

myth

Open and receptive leaders are not threatening

Leaders have power and power is threatening. Can you hire and fire? Do you deliver performance evaluations? Do you give or deny raises? Though you might not have a threatening style (and I hope you don't), you're intimidating merely as a result of your position.

You have power to the extent you have influence. To deny it would be irresponsible. To wield it for its own sake is also irresponsible. That fine line is what causes concern among conscientious people in high positions.

Story

Acknowledging his power, a very bright department head told his staff that he knew it was risky for them to give him feedback, report problems, and admit mistakes. He also acknowledged that it was only over time that he could prove it was safe to share, so he suggested they start with smaller issues. With some trepidation, they made suggestions and occasionally questioned him.

Though he couldn't always respond the way they wished, he thanked them for their feedback and consistently got back to them.

Now they sometimes forget his position. He delights in this because he realizes that he and the company are gaining far more than he would ever lose.

Confidence
Stress
Time Management

myth

It should be lonely at the top

Is it supposed to be isolating because it's the trade-off for status and a higher salary? There are many clichés implying that top executives should go it alone, such as "The buck stops here." For some reason, there is reluctance to lessening the isolation, even though it increases the stress of high-ranking staff.

Story

Whenever this CEO was in the office saying to himself, "What am I going to do?" or "I wonder what he was thinking?" or "How did she decide that?" or "Why did they do it that way?" we suggested he use this trigger thought: "Why am I just asking myself these questions?"

He began calling in relevant staff to provide information and suggestions. This not only elevated the morale of the people who had so conscientiously served him, but he also found that his final decisions were much better and that buy-in was no longer a hard sell.

He also remembered to let "his advisors" know when he decided not to take their input and, for the most part, they understood, or at least accepted it. They didn't need him to always take their advice, but they did need to know why it was rejected so they, too, could learn from the experience.

myth

Perfectionism is a worthy goal

I question whether it could ever be a goal since it is, by definition, impossible to reach and may even be a form of success-sabotage.

Many self-described perfectionists admit to being frustrated and unhappy. They know almost nothing is ever going to be perfect and that they're never going to feel like they've accomplished what they set out to do, so of course they're going to be disheartened and rarely satisfied.

Story

Because he was a perfectionist, the boss imposed his expectations on to his direct reports. Nothing they did was ever good enough. No one ever got a 5 on a performance evaluation. There was always a "but" after a rare compliment. The impossibly high expectations spread throughout the company and were, therefore, out of reach for everyone. The workplace became tense and frustrating and somewhat depressing.

He knew that to change anything, he had to face up to what he was doing to himself. It had been a lifelong struggle to accept reality, which usually didn't match his definition of perfect. He knew he'd have a hard time changing his way of looking at the world, but he also recognized that it was a corrosive leadership style.

He finally decided to share his inner struggle with his employees. He told them he was having a hard time getting out of his own way, but that he wanted to try lightening up when it came to them. He acknowledged it would be difficult for him and that he wouldn't always be successful, i.e. less than perfect.

As long as he was willing to try, the employees were happy to give him a chance. They tell him that his attempts are the perfect anecdote to perfectionism, which helps him smile when he slips.

myth

Selfishness is always bad

There is good kind of selfishness. It ensures that professionals are happy in their jobs and achieving satisfaction, which is different from exploiting others. Healthy selfishness means that people feel comfortable acknowledging what's in it for them.

We know that for those in the "helping professions," the best way they can be of service to others is to take care of themselves. Surely this is good advice for every employment sector.

Story

Like most hospitals, the entire focus of the staff was helping patients. From the medical personnel to the cafeteria to the gift shop to the administration - it was all about providing service to patients and their families. The focus was so outwardly directed that there was a certain amount of pervasive guilt if any time was spent looking inward.

When the HR director began reading about the perils of Vicarious Trauma and Compassion Fatigue - reliving one's own experience when witnessing other people's trauma and the cumulative effect of hearing painful stories - she decided it was time to support those who support.

She set up ongoing stress-reduction groups to deal with specific issues and offered everyone exercise, yoga, and massage sessions. They expanded their Employee Assistance Program, urging people to access counseling when feeling the need.

The message was clear. "Take care of yourself so you can take care of others."

myth

Most people who are promoted, appointed, or hired for high positions feel ready and competent

In truth, the "Impostor Syndrome" is common and honest people will acknowledge that they experience it. They struggle with self-talk that says, "I can't believe I was hired and they think I can do the job!" or "Why would they promote me? I don't know enough."

Story

I have talked with many newly appointed CEOs who worry, behind the closed door of their beautiful offices, that they'll be "found out" and everyone will realize that they're not up to the task. Similar stories came from administrators in almost every field, newly promoted supervisors, and recently elected officials.

I'm sure medical professionals have the same misgivings. I just don't want to know. I picture a surgeon standing over my anesthetized body saying, "Wow. She thinks I can take out her appendix!"

Everyone is new at one time. Honest leaders will admit to feelings of confusion and fear of incompetence. If shared, those admissions go a long way toward encouraging loyal assistance from their employees.

myth

New supervisors should pretend to be confident and knowledgeable even when they're not

No one can be the new person in the group and have as much information as the veterans so it's best that you sit back and listen, learn from your employees, and ask naive questions. If you acknowledge your dependence on the staff, they'll be delighted to help. Pretend you don't need them and important information may be withheld.

Story

Feeling a little inadequate, a newly hired upper-level manager swaggered into the department and indicated that he would be making some changes to increase efficiency. The employees silently balked and resisted. Because he didn't seem interested in their wisdom or experience, they didn't share it and soon things began to go downhill.

He finally received some coaching and advice. As a result, he called a meeting and admitted that he'd been premature, had not put enough trust in the staff, and needed to learn from them.

Because most people are forgiving, they thanked him for his honesty and immediately and continually came to his aid. They shared all they knew and offered assistance, proving that people are happy to help when given the opportunity.

myth

Public Speaking comes easily to most people

If you experience speaker anxiety, you have company: studies report that fear of death is second in line to the fear of public speaking, so apparently many people would rather die than speak publicly! In one of my Public Speaking workshops, a participant observed, "So the person delivering the eulogy would rather be in the casket?"

Story

When I ask what people fear most about speaking publicly, the responses fall into four categories: making a mistake, going blank, looking nervous, and audience members falling asleep.

From years of experience and my share of mess-ups, I can assure you that audiences are very forgiving and supportive if you acknowledge your mistakes and comfortably move on. They can easily become uncomfortable, however, if you get upset, angry, or embarrassed after making an error.

A few hints that help:
- If you're uncomfortable looking into people's eyes, look at the back wall; it will appear as though you're looking at the audience.
- Frequently move your head and body to include all attendees.
- Podiums are a barrier, so consider keeping your notes in your hand or on a small table.
- If you have a PowerPoint, narrate the content, but try not to read it verbatim.
- Make an attempt at informality.

As simple as it seems, the best way to get over speaker's anxiety is to just keep speaking!

myth

Strength is measured by a lack of emotion

How is it that stoicism is equated with strength? How did emotion and weakness become synonymous?

There is a fear that an emotional reaction will prevent a proper and professional response. Are we so untrusting of our colleagues that we think sharing our feelings will render us vulnerable? In fact, nothing exhibits trust more than the willingness to be exposed.

Unfortunately, women more often report feeling the need to suppress emotion so they don't invite gender stereotyping or sexism. Did women work so hard to get this far to not be themselves? There is a choice to either play into a stereotype or change it. One way to change this one, is to show that emotion and professionalism are not mutually exclusive.

Story

A business owner, known for his stoic and emotionless style, had to tell his workforce that economics required downsizing by a third. He rented a theater so that he could tell everyone at once.

He approached the podium and looked out at his loyal staff. Much to everyone's surprise - and his own - he burst out crying. He left the stage and returned moments later, only to cry again. The third time, he finally was able to make the dreaded announcement. Even those who lost their jobs said "At least he cares."

myth

Self-judgment keeps us accountable

How is this any different from being critical of others? Accountability is not synonymous with being judgmental. It's about recognizing what's happening and taking responsibility for fixing it.

Story

A few years ago, I began asking people what they remembered at the end of a workday. Invariably, they focused on the one mistake they'd made (regardless of its size), even though they had accomplished many good things the rest of the day.

Trust that you'll be responsible for your mistakes and conscientious about righting wrongs without having to beat yourself up.

myth

Stress is the result of hard work

Stress is not the result of hard work, it's the result of working hard and not accomplishing everything you want. If you have 10 things on your list and do all 10, you're not stressed, just tired. If you have 10 things on your list and only do 3, you have a gap. That gap is what causes stress.

It's not uncommon for people to say, "I didn't get anything done today," when they really mean they didn't accomplish what they had hoped.

Consider making a list at the end of the day that recounts all that you've done. I suspect it will be longer than your original "to do" list.

Story

People often say they don't get through their lists because they're constantly interrupted, so I ask whether "interruption" is on their list. It never is. If you added interruption for numbers 4, 7, and 11, every time someone interrupted, you could say "Wow! I thought I'd never get to that!" and check it off.

We often feel diverted by those we serve and consider them an interruption of our work rather than the reason for it. A teacher once told me that her curriculum would be perfect if it weren't for the students; a department store salesperson said, "We could keep the place so neat if the customers didn't keep coming and coming;" and my favorite was the group that complained about constantly being interrupted by calls.

They were a Call Center.

myth

Time can be managed

Time is a given. You can only manage your life within it.

There are a myriad of time management courses and systems offering great suggestions and models, but one size does not fit all. They only work if they're compatible with your style.

There are people who work best in an orderly fashion, finishing projects or reports days before the deadline; there are others who are only creative at the last minute and work right up to the deadline. Accepting who we are - and what works best with our particular style - eliminates the stress of constantly feeling inefficient and inadequate.

Story

Some years ago, a company invested money in a time management system for all its top level employees. It worked beautifully for some and not at all for others. When it was time for another round, they urged managers and supervisors to choose the system that best fit their individual styles.

Funds were provided to each person to attend the training of his or her choice, which resulted in the majority reporting personal improvement. Despite having to sort through and purchase multiple systems, the time and money spent turned out to be a sound investment.

myth

Managing conflicting priorities
is not that difficult

There are many who work for and/or answer to several individuals - sometimes their coworkers, sometimes their bosses, and sometimes people from other divisions. Everyone might be giving this person tasks and all of them might be asking for priority treatment.

Supervisors are certainly not sitting in a room conspiring to make the employee's life crazy, so the only one who can make everyone aware of what's going on is that person. You have to urge him/her to speak up.

Story

An administrative assistant worked for 3 bosses. The amount of work wasn't the problem, it was each boss saying: "Please do this now" or "This is top priority" or "I need this as soon as possible," so she thought that setting priorities was her burden.

She finally brought the supervisors together and told them that her life was too stressful and she needed more clarification to work effectively.

Now when there are overlapping priorities, she'll say to them, "I don't care what I do first, second, or third, but you have to decide among you how the assignments should be prioritized." She might also say "If I do this, I'll have to put aside your colleague's request," or if the dueling tasks come from the same person, she'll ask which one is more important.

myth

Priority lists should always be adhered to with preference given to the most important items

It makes intuitive sense, but sometimes we're not in the mood or don't have the resources to do what is most important, so it's really okay to do anything on the list - no matter what the priority - rather than do nothing at all.

Story

The management team was sent to a seminar on priority management. They came back with expensive systems that helped them clearly define what should be done first, second, and third. It worked great the first couple of weeks and then some people started cheating.

When they got together for a follow-up session, one man admitted that he wasn't always in the place to accomplish the highest priority and others agreed.

They adopted a "Do Something, Not Nothing" policy, even if the something was number 10 on the list. When asked why it felt better, the response was that the absence of guilt freed up more energy to accomplish the rest.

myth

I can only stop and talk with people when I have time

When would that be? Is there ever a good moment? Do you ever look like you have plenty of time to chat? Are people comfortable interrupting you?

There's usually more to be done in a day than there are hours to accomplish everything, so chances are that you sometimes appear inaccessible.

Story

A busy Department Head struggled to be responsive but clearly delivered the message - mainly through body language - that he didn't have time for conversation.

He was finally convinced that it wasn't the amount of time that was the issue; it was his inability to be 100% focused on the person talking to him.

He found when he gives his employees his undivided attention, they need less time. He says "I have only 5 minutes, but it's all yours," and if they need more time he schedules another meeting to continue the conversation.

Decision-Making
Problem-Solving

myth

All decisions should be made at high levels

How many times do employees think or say, "If they only asked me."?

Whenever decisions are made or problems need solving, the first question should be, "Who is missing from around the table?"

People who do the job every day know how to solve the problems, but they are often left out of the process because of their inferior status, so the managerial staff – armed with only partial information – risks coming up with the wrong solutions.

Story #1

A factory built a new machine designed painstakingly by their engineers at enormous cost. It didn't work. The employees on the plant floor said, "We knew it wouldn't work, but they never asked us."

The engineers now bring in relevant staff from the outset. They've learned that operators using the machines have information essential to the design process. Support and customer service staff understand the ramifications of faulty equipment, and purchasing and maintenance staff knows what happens when there is too much scrap. They no longer design anything without the stakeholders being around the table.

Story #2

When consulting in areas of customer service improvement, it's usually the top leadership that's sitting around the table. The first question I ask is "Where's the receptionist?" Since that person is often at the bottom of the organizational chart, I'm met with puzzled looks. But who knows more about how customers are feeling than the person who answers the phone or is the first to see them coming through the door?

myth

The design of workspaces is the responsibility of the leadership team, architect, or space planner

Staff members are the ones who know the space requirements, who needs to be near whom, and what logistical and privacy issues affect them. They should be included throughout the design process for two reasons: They know what they need to work efficiently and they'll embrace the floor plan they helped design.

Story

While working with a municipality that decided to merge several departments and move everyone to a space that was being renovated for them, I suggested an exercise where those directly affected could figure out who should be located where by negotiating with each other, taking into account issues of required proximity, environmental needs, and efficiency. We made life size cut outs of the furniture and they had a wonderful time moving them around the huge empty room.

They came up with what they deemed the perfect physical layout for their purposes and the experience served as a team building exercise that resulted in the group coalescing much earlier than they would have if administrators had created the design.

Predictably, some decisions didn't turn out well, but the staff owned them and had permission to make further changes.

myth

Good or bad decisions
should be assessed by the outcome

Outcomes are affected by chance, luck, unanticipated occurrences, and new information, which is why the outcome isn't necessarily a good indicator of whether your decision-making process was sound.

You can, however, make sure that the approach is sound and that decisions are based on thorough research and well-thought-out projections and anticipated results. That's really all you can do.

If there is a negative outcome, assessment should be based on the amount of thought and inquiry that preceded the decision. If the evaluation reveals that everything was in fact taken into account, then there is no need for negative self-judgement. There may, however, be a need for more assessment.

Story

Imagine that you wanted to buy a house and you had all the required tests done. A few years later, your area has an uncharacteristic tornado and the home is seriously damaged. You might think that your decision to purchase was a bad one, but it wouldn't be true. Based on what you knew at the time, your decision-making process was good.

Conversely, you wanted the house so badly that you did the minimal amount of checking and testing. 30 years later, the house is standing tall. Was the decision to buy a good one? Not really. Your process was flawed and you just lucked out.

myth

There is such a thing as No Decision

No decision is a decision to keep things the same, to maintain the status quo. It's a decision to change nothing.

You might say, "I haven't decided whether to buy a new car," but you actually have because you continue to drive the old one.

When it seems like we're indecisive, we should look at the potential losses and other ramifications of not moving forward.

Story

A frustrated leadership team asked for outside guidance because though they were excited about the company's potential for growth, week after week they refused to take the steps needed to make it happen. They found themselves losing self-esteem as a group.

With the help of the facilitator, they finally recognized that their so-called indecision was a choice to keep things the same because they didn't want to face the downsides of expansion. It freed them up to make and discuss the issues: potentially more staff, higher budgets, movement from a family-feeling company to a more corporate environment, extra training, disruption of well-oiled working groups, and changes in supervisory responsibilities.

In other words, increased success had its trade-offs, but this revelation set them free so they could make the hard decisions about whether to keep some things the same or to take significant leaps that required putting support systems in place.

myth

Final solutions don't need to be revisited

There is a sociological term called Unintended Consequences, which means that solving one problem creates others. Not anticipating collateral consequences is a fairly common occurrence, especially if we don't think long term.

There are endless societal examples. There are also numerous situations in the workplace exemplified by a change being made in one department causing problems in another.

Story

One clear example happened in a manufacturing plant when the finance department changed various due dates for reports. It made their lives much easier, but the negative reaction was loud and clear because the new dates bumped up against production and shipping deadlines, thus not allowing enough time to gather the information finance required.

In the same way developers have to go through an environmental impact process, the company decided they'd use a similar model. Whenever any department wanted to alter something that might affect other parts of the company, they allowed time for everyone to evaluate the impact of the changes.

Not only did frustration and anger diminish, but they also learned about and appreciated how other departments operated. One woman put it beautifully. "We seem like one company now, not several under the same roof."

myth

Announcing a well-thought-out decision should be enough to ensure buy-in

After much deliberation and hard work coming to a decision, it's not unusual for leadership to be disappointed by the tepid reception from the rest of the staff.

If you keep in mind that they didn't go through your process of research, discussion, and final decision-making, you'll understand why they don't immediately embrace your conclusions. When you finally get around to informing them, remember that they are now where you started, not where you've arrived. Find a way to bring them up to speed so they're comfortable accepting the outcome.

Story

An employee committee took on the daunting task of developing workplace guidelines. They met for months, researching various models and arguing certain points from a multitude of perspectives. It was a tough job and they finally emerged with a new employee handbook that they proudly debuted at an all-staff meeting.

As questions and comments were entertained from the audience, the committee members were both surprised and somewhat annoyed that so much of the conversation was about topics the committee had discussed weeks ago.

They soon realized that because no one else in the company had benefitted from their deliberative process, they would of course be in the dark and therefore have questions.

Two things became apparent: to insure against a knowledge gap, they should have found a way to share their deliberations with everyone in the company, and they should have known that unquestioned acceptance of their recommendations was unlikely.

myth

Decisions to downsize
should only be made by high-ranking leaders

Cutting employees is certainly traumatic for the people being fired, but it's also difficult for the survivors. They stand to lose their friends and colleagues, and they find themselves waiting for "the other shoe to drop," wondering if they'll be next. Morale decreases and guilt is pervasive. Stress increases. Productivity goes down.

Before taking that major and agonizing step of letting people go, leaders should discuss it with their employees. Throughout the country, people are coming up with creative and innovative ways to preserve jobs for themselves and their colleagues. It's been heartening to hear stories of employees cooperating in ways that were never imagined.

Story

Faced with declining sales and frightening projections, the management team was moving toward layoffs. One department head suggested that they share the forecast with the employees and ask for their opinions.

The employees were so flattered to be involved that they set into motion a series of meetings focused on the doomsday report. In the end, there were no layoffs because they collectively found ways to be more efficient and frugal, volunteered to take pay cuts, gave up some fringe benefits for a year, restructured their work so that retired positions need not be immediately filled, initiated savings for small and large expenditures, and embraced the responsibility of entrepreneurship and marketing

myth

Budgets should be dictated from above

Do we really believe that employees don't have any ideas about how to save money or reduce waste, or the best way to allocate resources?

They often know more than those at the top.

Story

With the economy going south, the leadership team decided to share the financial status of the company with all the employees. They designed an intranet program that reported the current financial situation on a day-to-day basis.

More importantly, they told the employees that if they could come up with viable ways to save money and not affect quality, they would be directly helping the company and indirectly ensuring their own security.

The suggestions poured in because at every level, employees finally had a legitimate avenue for sharing their ideas. The money saved was enormous and the conversation continued after the crisis as they talked about efficiencies and ways to enhance the quality of the product.

Again they proved that the people who do the job every day are the organization's experts.

myth

Arriving at consensus
is not worth the time it takes

Majority rule is definitely quicker. You vote, and if at least 51% agree, the matter is settled. But keep in mind that you risk 49% of the people being unhappy and often downright disgruntled. They may follow through begrudgingly, ignore the changes or, worse, sabotage the decision.

Consensus does take time at the outset, but once the decision is made, little or no further time is required. Reaching a consensus means that everyone has the chance to discuss the issues and then agrees to "live" with the decision. It may not be a first choice, but individuals are truly okay with it, and you are close to 100% unanimity as you move forward.

Juries work that way. Imagine 12 jurors. 11 are leaning in one direction and the negotiations continue. True consensus does not mean that eleven people wait patiently, or impatiently, for the "holdout" to agree with them. It may mean that the 11 will move closer to the one person's point-of-view after hearing his or her arguments.

Story

A successful non-profit committed to true consensus for every decision from major strategic plans to what kind of coffee to stock in the kitchen. It was sometimes crazy-making and there were a couple of new hires along the way who simply couldn't stand it and left. They found it time-consuming and exhausting.

Though the staff teased themselves occasionally, they described the environment as all-inclusive. As one longtime employee said, "Though there are complaints about the process, there are few complaints about the results. We know we're unusual and are proud of it."

myth

It's easy to identify fundamental problems

The reason solutions sometimes don't work is that either the problem was misstated or the right causes weren't identified.

Have you ever engaged the so-called "Cause and Effect" exercise? A problem is stated, then you work backwards answering the question: "What causes that?" Each time you get an answer, you ask the same question: "What causes that?" until there is no longer an answer, at which point you've pinpointed the basic problem. Typically, it's not the one initially identified.

Story

Having seen this exercise work numerous times, I'm hooked. Here is one of many examples: The problem initially identified was low productivity. The "What causes that?" questions elicited the following series of possible reasons: systemic issues, ineffective employees, an inefficient building, lack of materials, money crunch, poor planning, and poor communication.

Systemic issues were a result of poor documentation and ineffective employees a result of low morale. Building inefficiencies resulted from not changing the layout of the physical space even though their workforce had tripled, and the lack of materials happened because of a money crunch and lack of planning. Ultimately, the final answer boiled down to a "lack of communication and inadequate time devoted to discovering root causes."

They changed their structure and created a communication process that included the entire workforce, and productivity immediately began to increase. Had they not participated in the Cause and Effect exercise they may have borrowed more money, fired people, moved, or stocked up on materials they didn't need.

myth

Employees should only raise problems if they have solutions to offer

"To stop the whining and complaining," said one CEO, "we tell our employees that if they want to report a problem, they should also suggest a way to resolve it."

Often reinforced by signs saying "Don't bring me problems if you can't offer solutions," this off-putting and all too common policy has resulted in perfectly reasonable people ceasing to bring up important issues if they don't have a resolution in mind.

As a result, problems don't surface when they should and often get worse when they might have been solved early on.

Story

A CEO had a sign on his door that read, "I don't want to hear about it unless you can tell me how to fix it!" so no one told him anything. With the lack of information, the problems grew worse and he eventually blew up when he found out about them because it was almost too late to engage in remediation.

On quick reflection, he realized it was his own policy that had created the dilemma and that he was now caught in its unreasonableness. He had no immediate solution and was therefore not supposed to bring up the problem.

He shared that epiphany with the employees. The signs came down and people started coming forth with observations. Where there were no immediate fixes, they brainstormed possibilities.

myth

Employees are only interested in their major suggestions being implemented

Little things often make a big difference, so make sure to address the easily implemented suggestions (the "low hanging fruit") within two weeks of hearing them.

For those that take longer to implement, let people know that they're being worked on, and when you finally put them into practice, acknowledge whose idea it was. Lastly, as soon as you reject a suggestion, share the reasons why.

Employee surveys are often perceived as an effort designed to "pretend to care," so be sure to invite responses only if you value your employee's opinions and plan to implement what you can.

Story

Asking for input, the executive team was overwhelmed with ideas - little and big. The temptation was to put them all aside until major changes could be made. Fortunately they decided to choose those things that could be put into place right away, even though many of them were small and incremental.

The employees were thrilled and felt that the quick response meant that other, more major innovations would happen down the road. When they did, the staff felt respected even though some of their ideas didn't make it. There was an update every few weeks listing what had been done, what might be done, and what would not be done with accompanying reasons.

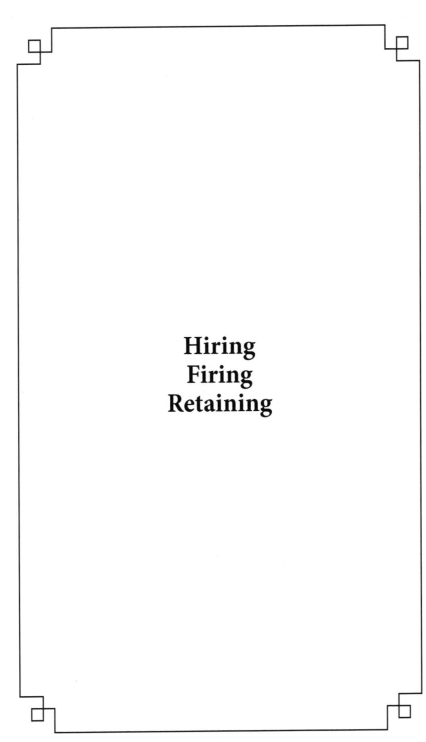

Hiring
Firing
Retaining

myth

Hiring should be the job
of leadership and HR only

It's not just about bringing in new people; it's also about easily assimilating and integrating the new hires so that they're able to perform well from the outset. To make sure that the right people are brought on, organizations are increasingly involving staff in the hiring process.

Remember the game we played as kids when everyone locked arms in a circle and some child had to try to break in? That's what it feels like for new employees unless their peers are part of the hiring process. When the existing team has input, they won't lock arms but will stand on their heads to assimilate the new person. They'll enthusiastically train them and help aid their development because they have some responsibility for their being there.

Human Resources has an important role in starting the process, checking and not sharing confidential information, and engaging in the initial screening. Beyond that, consider bringing the prospective employees' colleagues together to take part in the interview process.

Story

A rather large manufacturing plant required 30% more employees because of a new product ramp-up. The HR Director had heard from colleagues in other companies that the peers of potential hires were included in the interview process, so with some trepidation she gave it a try.

HR did the initial screening and fact checking. Then half the departments followed the traditional interviewing procedures using only supervisors. The other half included team members and after they met the candidates, they submitted their choices in order of priority. Practically all the recommendations were taken.

Three years later, the latter group boasted a much higher retention rate.

myth

Hiring interviews cover almost everything there is to know about a job

Most interviews with potential new hires are not based on "truth in advertising." It's common to emphasize the benefits and positive aspects of the position you're trying to fill while leaving out the downsides such as required overtime, stressful periods, and customer/employee tensions.

Story

Observing a series of interviews with job candidates, I noticed that almost all the reasons former employees left the job were omitted in the position description. I asked the interview team why they hadn't been as forthright about the problem areas as they were about the positive aspects of the positions. All three replied, "We'll lose the best prospects!"

That may have been true, but it's far better for people to self-select out before being hired than for them to leave in frustration a few months into it after a lot of time, energy, and money has been devoted to their training and orientation.

How do you know that the people you bring on can handle the challenges if you don't make them aware of them from the beginning? People who leave early in their tenure often say, "This isn't what I signed on for!"

Hiring right is the best indicator of retention.

myth

Frequently revisiting job descriptions is unnecessary

Despite best efforts to clarify job descriptions, the work world changes regularly. What seemed descriptive last year may not make sense any more. Job descriptions should be checked against actual duties performed, and then re-evaluated on a regular basis, and not just by HR. Ask the employees how they spend their time and what they actually do. To be sure the organization is run efficiently, you might also want to ask if the designated duties make sense.

Story

Periodically the team comes together to make a list of everything that needs to be done. They ask if the tasks were assigned by skill and interest or whether they remained someone's responsibility because no one had ever bothered to change them.

As a group, they reassign duties and often find that because people are now focusing on what they do best and what makes the most sense for their positions, they are enjoying themselves more and are much more successful. Efficiency, productivity, and job satisfaction have risen to new levels.

Having so much success in the office, several people tried it with the chore list at home. They found that if someone chose to clean the bathroom, the chances that it would be spotless were much better than if it were assigned to a family member who didn't care. Like the workplace, cross-training is necessary and even appreciated but, for the most part, everyone is doing what they excel at most of the time.

myth

It's too costly to overlap outgoing employees with new hires

The cost of overlapping the departing employee with the incoming person for training purposes is far less than a new hire trying to learn the job in isolation. Consider the time and money saved when the person doing the job is able to transfer information (both on a large and small scale) to his or her replacement.

Story

The company had a large cohort of people who would soon retire. To save money, the policy was to ask replacements to arrive the day after the veteran employees left. There was always an enormous learning curve, and everyone expected it to be 6 months to a year before the new hires were completely up to speed.

As an experiment, they decided to try keeping some retirees on with their replacements for 1 month. It wasn't an easy decision because of the expense and because they were concerned that it would be unnatural to have two people filling one position.

The extent to which there was an upside was unanticipated. Duel salaries more than made up for the early high performance levels of the new employees. Not only did the veterans understand the workplace culture, roles, processes, vocabulary, systemic issues, and whom to go to for what, but they also appreciated the nuances of their jobs. By the time the transition took place, it felt like the new employees had been there for years

myth

Orientation for new hires
should be designed by veteran employees

Long-time employees can't remember what they didn't know when they came on board. It's the new people who easily recall the missing information that might have facilitated their entry.

Story

The Human Resources Department brought together employees hired in the last 6 months and asked them what would have helped them assimilate more quickly into the organization. They were stunned by the long list of simple questions such as where to put their lunch and how to find certain files, and larger issues such as the cultural norms and vocabulary peculiar to their organization.

Now they have an online glossary that explains the numerous acronyms and terms. They've added staff photos and short bios as well as their job descriptions and who to go to for what. All orientations are led by a duo - a veteran employee from HR and a relatively new employee who can relate.

myth

When budgets are tight, training is expendable

During tough times, one easy, short-term solution is to eliminate training, but it puts employees at a great disadvantage and it may hurt customers and clients.

Story

Like so many companies, training was high on the deletion list until one of the Managing Directors said, "I heard that companies that continue training and advertising during the recession fare better when the recession lifts."

Everyone agreed that it made intuitive sense, but as one person said, "It's so easy to do without and it doesn't hurt anyone now." The question was whether it would hurt employees and those they served in the future. Would they fall behind and be unable to catch up even as their finances improved?

The answer could only be speculative, but it caused them to pause. Finally, someone said, "What if we commit to continued training and look for less expensive ways to do it?"

They used their in-house experts, went to online web delivery to save money on travel, and committed one person to continually look for training options that weren't costly. They also vowed to expand training programs when budgets improved.

myth

A reduced workforce leads
to a new, leaner model that should be embraced

But at what cost? As a result of downsizing during tough economic times, the remaining workforce usually takes on other duties and works longer hours under more pressure. That's why those retaining their positions deserve a lot of attention and gratitude. They're doing what they have to do, mostly without complaint, because they know it's necessary.

But what happens when the economy turns around and a smaller workforce is no longer required? We're finding that some at the top are saying: "Our numbers are up and we're doing better, so let's not add back more people. Our employees seem to be functioning just fine despite the reduced staffing levels."

Story

One company was in exactly that position and leadership showed little concern about employee stress, pending burnout, and the fact that people felt taken advantage of when business increased and there was little desire to bring back the required staff.

Employees felt that it was unethical and unkind to take advantage of those who had stepped up to the plate in a time of need. The decision-makers seemed to be turning a blind eye to exhausted staff that were afraid to say anything lest they be considered disloyal. The leaders were hurting those who had enthusiastically helped.

When confronted, the leadership team said "But we've been operating this way for some time." "But at what cost?" said the employee representatives. "At what cost?"

Fortunately, two of the top tier finally said, "You're right. Give us time to work this out." Their colleagues were, at first, furious and the leadership meeting lasted for hours. Near the end, one of the VPs said, "I wonder if our workforce feels like I feel now. If they're this tired and worn out, we're going to lose them when the market resurges. It's going to be our fault.

The rehiring process started the next day.

myth

Downsizing to save money
is the best decision during tough times

It may be a short-term solution, but when times get better, your skilled staff will not be there and you'll have to hire new people and train them at considerable cost. So, yes, it is an immediate way to save money, but what's the expense of ramping up again when the economy improves?

We are notoriously sacrificing the long term for the short term.

Story

During tough times when revenues are severely reduced, there are some brave companies that have chosen not to let anyone go. Instead everyone pitches in to make renovations and repairs and to help with landscaping and a variety of other chores until the market turns around.

More than one of the CEO's has indicated that this is not just about altruism. It's about good business. When the economy improves, all their qualified employees will still be there, ready to roll. In every case the employees were grateful to management for creatively employing them and remained extremely loyal and totally committed to the company's success.

myth

Calling it downsizing or reorganizing helps ease the pain

You might as well call it "euphemizing." It may be marginally relieving for people to know that they were not let go for cause, but the truth is, they're out of a job: no money, no benefits, no security, and it's a blow to their professional identity.

So, in truth, calling it downsizing or reorganizing may make you feel better, but it doesn't help them.

Story

Listening to the reactions of victims (and yes, they are victims) of economic downturns is illustrative. More than one person articulated some version of the following: "Telling me I've been 'downsized' or that I'm losing my job because my company is 'reorganizing' doesn't help. They need to face the fact that their decision means I can't pay my mortgage or my kid's tuition, buy groceries, or keep my car.

"Those fancy words might make the bosses feel better when they give us the ax, but they sure as hell don't help those of us who are at their mercy."

Difficult as it may be, try to be sensitive to euphemistic verbiage. Tell the truth, exhibit meaningful empathy, and set up a system that offers as much help as possible to those you're letting go

myth

You don't have to worry about how you treat people during an economic downturn because they can't afford to leave

You may get away with treating people any way you want when there are fewer opportunities available elsewhere, but once the economy improves, those who have not been treated well are more likely to jump ship in search of a more compassionate employer.

Whatever rationale you may have for acting insensitively during this short term will cost you in the long run. You'll have to replace previously loyal employees with unknowns who need training and you'll have a bad rep on the street, which might affect your ability to recruit in the future. So why wouldn't you be nice regardless of the state of the economy?

Story

Kindness did not come naturally to this CEO, so he feigned it when he couldn't afford to lose anyone. But when the recession hit, he let down his guard and, true to his nature, was downright unpleasant. No one left his employ because they were desperate to have jobs, but when the market improved, he lost many of his well-trained workers.

He has since learned two lessons: his reputation (which he is working hard to repair) was legendary and affected his ability to hire good people, and it takes the same amount of time to be nice as it does to be unkind.

myth

Survivors of a recession
should just be happy they have jobs

Though they may be grateful, they're probably also struggling with survivors' guilt and the loss of their colleagues and friends. They're doing more work to pick up the slack - often out of their areas of expertise - and worrying that their own job security may be in question.

Story

A company downsized by almost a third. When the President and VPs noticed that the remaining employees seemed unhappy, their response was, "What's your problem? You have your jobs!" The survivors were thereafter afraid to express concerns, and the risk that serious work-related mistakes would go unreported was at an all-time high.

Luckily, their HR person was both sensitive and assertive. She reminded management that the employees couldn't celebrate their good fortune when their friends and co-workers were being laid off, leaving them with even more work for which they had little or no training.

The bosses reluctantly listened. They gathered everyone over pizza and encouraged them to talk about how hard it was to see their workmates leave. They generated a list of needed training tools with a plan to use both in-house and outside trainers, and invited people to come forth about concerns without risk of jeopardizing their positions.

The isolation that had developed began to slowly disappear and employees report that they're beginning to heal.

Change

myth

Only negative change is stressful

Positive change can be just as stressful as negative change because with every gain, there is a loss. There is almost always a trade-off.

Try this. Fold your hands and notice which thumb is on top. Now unfold and refold them with the other thumb on top. Fold your arms. Notice what arm is on top. Now unfold and refold them with the other arm on top. It's probably uncomfortable. These are small, simple exercises, but they're challenging because you're giving up the familiar.

Story

When my husband was in graduate school, I worked in a tough part of a city fraught with gangs and drug addicts. I said to this guy (please remember I was young and naïve), "You have to stop using heroin. It's going to kill you." He replied, "Gee, I wish someone had told me that before." (Speaking of "Duh!"….)

He then explained that if he got off drugs, he'd have to leave his neighborhood, his friends, his family, and create a new identity. He had a long list of trade-offs, none of which included the high or the addiction. It was the first of many times that I realized you don't gain anything without giving something up.

There are endless stories emerging from organizations depicting shocked administrators who tried to implement what they thought was a very positive change, only to meet with resistance. The smart ones stopped insisting that the "new way" should be embraced, and instead asked employees to identify the issues and offer some suggestions to make the transitions easier. They were encouraged to list the trade-offs and talk about the downside as well as the upside.

The executives were surprised by the range of very helpful solutions offered, such as increased training, allowing time to adjust, and paying attention to the effect on other departments.

myth

"If you aren't willing to change, perhaps you don't belong here" is a great way to motivate people to get on board

On the contrary, it's an effective way to encourage employees to keep their concerns to themselves. Change brings up the fear of the unknown, control issues, loss of the familiar, and anxiety. If you're thinking that none of these emotions belongs in the workplace, where do you suggest they go?

Story

The President and Vice Presidents of the company enthusiastically put signs up challenging people to "change or get off the bus." The bus analogy reminded me of brave Rosa Parks and discrimination, but beyond that, I asked if they were expecting their employees would embrace change and keep their fears and concerns to themselves.

They met with focus groups to discuss the numerous proposed changes. The meetings were very emotional and cathartic. Employees began to help one another and came up with ways to manage the changes while addressing their concerns.

It was still a struggle, but being assured that they would not be "fired for feeling" allowed them to be creative.

myth

We've always done it that way,
so there's no need to change

Many workplace procedures and processes may have been instituted for good reasons that are no longer valid. Consistency certainly has its perks, but it can also be the last resort of the unimaginative. Make certain that all routines are periodically reviewed to ensure that they are still practical, cost-effective, and necessary.

Story

A couple was preparing a pot roast. Before putting it in the oven the man cut off the end. His partner asked him why, and he said he wasn't sure but that his mother always did it. So they called Mom, only to find out that she was just doing what grandma did.

They all got in the car, went to the retirement home, and asked Grandma why she cut off the end of the roast. She said "I don't know why you do it. I did it because my pan was too small."

Routines may no longer be applicable for any number of reasons, so be grateful when someone questions them.

myth

You can force people to change their values

If they care about the consequences, you might be able to force people to change their behavior, but because values are so interconnected, changing them takes much more effort.

Story

I was at a party a few nights before an election. A very bright woman said, "I've voted a straight ticket for 25 years. I hate that I have to do that again this year because I can't stand most of the people running in my party."

"For Heaven's sake, don't vote for them," said a surprised guest.

"I have to," she said. "I've always voted a straight ticket."

People were on this woman - cajoling, teasing, hassling. After 10 minutes of harassment she said, "Hey, if I don't vote a straight ticket for the first time in 25 years, I have to look at everything else I'm doing in my life and I'm not ready to do that."

She understood that her values were intertwined and that if she reevaluated how she was voting, she'd have to question other strongly held beliefs.

When changes are aligned with our own value system they're easy for us to accommodate, but others may need time to adjust.

myth

Continuous Improvement has an end date

I know, I know. This sounds like a joke, but the following actually occurred.

Story

I happened to be facilitating a meeting with the CEO and his Vice Presidents when one of the VPs said, "What's with this Continuous Improvement effort? The damn thing never ends!"

"But it's called Continuous Improvement!" said a colleague.

"I know," he said, "but you'd think it would be over by now."

It turned out that the employees were also resistant because whenever an "improvement" was suggested, they felt they were being criticized for what they used to do.

"Are you saying that how we've operated for the last 15 years was wrong or a waste of time?" "Are you criticizing our judgment?" "We weren't good enough the way we were?"

Everyone finally embraced the process when it was clearly explained that the former way of doing things was based on old technology and information and that the improvements were not an indictment but a way to keep up with the times.

myth

Strategic Planning is an organized effort following well-defined steps

If done right, strategic planning is a messy process. At the outset, it uncovers more questions than answers. It challenges who you are and who you want to be. It may also generate opposition, which is tempting to ignore, but a lot of information can be gathered from resistance.

The only reason to develop a strategic plan is to effect change. Regardless of whether change is positive or negative, it's stressful because with gains there are losses. You're giving up the familiar and heading toward the unknown, all of which has to be addressed before the plan is developed.

Story

The Executive Director was very organized and orderly. Following his lead, the administrative team embarked on a strategic plan and expected they'd go through the steps fairly quickly. On the very first day it felt like the effort had been completely derailed. The mission, vision, and values statements were questioned, as was their historical business philosophy.

Fortunately their facilitator suggested they be grateful that their agenda had been "messed up" because now, he said, "You're entering the most creative part of the process."

And it was. They learned more at that juncture than they could have ever gathered had they been on the same page from the outset. It wasn't easy for those whose linear styles were challenged, but even they realized the benefit early on. They now describe their Strategic Plan as so much better "thanks to the mavericks who got them off track."

myth

Strategic Plans should be developed exclusively by the Leadership Team

It is true that unless the senior leadership team is committed to seeing the entire process through, employees will think it was a useless and insincere exercise, perhaps even designed to manipulate them.

However, when the plan is designed solely by the people at the top, it will be a tough sell. Correctly done, the process should include everyone at every level of the organization. Thorough assessments will provide the necessary information to move forward, and predictably, a lot of unexpected data that enhances the plan will emerge from throughout the organization.

Story

The Corporation's Leadership Team created a new strategic plan every five years but checked in regularly to see if it was still relevant. They began noticing that certain pieces of the plan weren't working because a myriad of issues and concerns from many departments hadn't been taken into account.

They finally realized that more than just upper management had to be involved. They put together a strategic planning committee that was comprised of all leadership and representatives from every department and every level of the organization. All employees participated in a focus group.

Reevaluation showed that they remained on target much more often and for several years out.

myth

Strategic Plans can be created during a two day retreat

Strategic Plans should take more than two days, but it's rare that the appropriate time is allotted.

Ideally the pre-planning mode will take about a month, collecting information and creating the plan 6-12 months, and 3-5 years to fully implement it. Creating sub-groups from various departments and levels to facilitate the action steps ensures progress.

Keep in mind that strategic plans are written for defined periods so they need to be constantly re-visited. Company growth or decline, changing economic conditions, new competition, and many other variables require that plans be reviewed for relevancy on a regular basis.

Story

A group about to embark on the strategic planning process had reservations. "That's going to take too long; it's not what we signed up for. We just want a clean, well-organized strategic plan that works."

"Wanting it to work is the pivotal point," said the facilitator. "The only way to have an effective process is to take the time," so they reluctantly agreed, grumbling all the way.

But the next time? They signed right on. "The results are convincing," they said. "The time we spent made for a much better plan that actually works!"

myth

Succession planning should be reserved for top executive positions

That implies that the only important jobs are high level ones and that you can get along without the others. Every person is pivotal to the smooth running of the organization, which is why grooming successors at all levels is becoming the norm.

Preparing internal candidates rather than hiring from the outside ensures continuity, provides seamless integration, and smooths the transition process because training begins long before an employee is promoted. An outside person is far more expensive to train than an employee who holds the institutional history and knowledge that are the foundations of a well-functioning organization.

Story

A mid-sized firm decided that succession planning from within allowed choice from a talent pool that was already highly qualified.

This led to other unexpected benefits: employees felt that the company valued their growth and was providing opportunities for developing new skills and abilities while increasing the chances for job security.

Though the initial goal was to fill key leadership roles, it began working at all levels of the organization. It wasn't long before everyone embraced a learning model tied to a possible career path.

Employees are now ready for new roles, and when someone leaves, they can more easily step in with confidence.

Feedback
Motivation
Evaluation

myth

Employees know what is expected of them

Of course they do! Why wouldn't they? It's in their job description, they're told over and over, so how could they still not know what's expected?

Obviously, if employees continue to misunderstand what they're supposed to be doing, the person delivering the information has some responsibility for it not being clear.

We share information the way we best gather it. If we're auditory learners, we tell someone what we want. If we're visual learners, we write out instructions. If we're experiential learners, we show people how to do it.

Delivering information in at least these 3 major modalities provides us a better chance of being understood correctly. We can't count on employees telling us their preferences because they may not completely understand their own styles or they don't dare suggest to their bosses how to effectively do their jobs.

Story

Gallup reported in the "2013 State of the American Workplace Report" that 70 percent of US workers are not reaching their full potential and are "not engaged" or are "actively disengaged" at their jobs. One of the reasons may be that they don't have a clear expectation of what their supervisors expect from them, even as supervisors think they're being clear.

My experience is that in those organizations where leaders vow to communicate their expectations in a modality tailored to each employee's method of learning, immediate results are impressive. They report that the level of understanding increases dramatically and that employees are extremely appreciative and more productive.

myth

If employees are not being reprimanded, they should assume their performance is acceptable

But they don't. If you say nothing one way or the other, they wonder and worry, so why keep positive feedback a secret? If people are doing a good job, you should tell them. If they're not, you should tell them that, too.

Story

A self-described "old school boss" regularly tells his employees that "no news is good news," so if they don't hear any criticism from him, they can assume he's happy. The problem with this is when he comes to work not smiling, or he locks himself in his office for a long time and doesn't talk to anybody, his employees automatically assume that they've done something wrong.

Since he doesn't always know he's coming across that way, he doesn't think to tell them that his unhappiness, his exclusion, or his being quiet has nothing to do with them.

He's improved a bit. Issuing compliments is hard for him, but he's learning and the response has been so positive that he's trying to be more forthcoming about the good work his employees are doing.

myth

Telling employees that they're your greatest asset is enough

Are they included in decisions and asked for their input? Do they have more, or at least as much, status as your customers? Does enough deserved praise come their way?

Story

The Executive Director was always saying "We're a family" and "Our employees are our first priority," which sounded nice but that's not how the employees saw it. "We are first after all the clients, all the other agencies, and anyone who happens to walk through the door!"

When a long-time employee decided to leave, he pointed out all the ways that what was said didn't match what was actually going on.

HR listened to him and the Leadership Team listened to her. They held a series of meetings and found that the former employee's assessment was shared by many. A committee of representatives from every department made it their mission to resolve the disparity and "walk the talk."

They're now a few years out and that committee, called The Recognizing and Rectifying Discrepancies Group, still exists.

myth

All forms of honest feedback are good

Feedback is only worthwhile if people can do something about it. Telling someone that s/he is too tall is not good feedback, but we say that kind of thing all the time: "Change your attitude," or "You have to be more conscientious," or " You have to try harder." Do people know exactly what to do? How do they know where to start? How will achievement be measured?

Feedback should be specific. Employees have the right to know how their progress will be assessed. "Being on time is a reflection of conscientiousness." "When you talk with customers, it's important that you lower your voice." "If you meet your deadlines, I'll know that you're trying harder."

Story

It's heartbreaking when a supervisor tells an employee that s/he has a lot of room for improvement. The person works hard to change 5 things and finds out that it was a 6th to which the boss was referring.

Many Performance Evaluations have general categories such as "Attitude" and "Conscientiousness," but if they don't require narrative explanations, you might as well be telling employees that they're too tall.

Good documentation requires more than broad statements that aren't useful. Comments should be exact and descriptive so that employees have a road map for improvement.

myth

We only talk behind people's backs when we're saying something negative

We actually talk behind people's backs in positive ways more often. The waiter leaves and we say to each other "Isn't he a great waiter?" We tell our family about how well the new colleague is working out, or coworkers comment on the terrific job someone is doing when the person isn't in the room.

One of the reasons we don't praise people face-to-face, is that it's hard to accept compliments in American culture, so we don't often give them.

Story

An executive director decided to implement the following: If someone says to a colleague, "We have this great new hire," or "Didn't so-and-so do a wonderful job on the project?" or "My assistant makes it possible for me to be productive," the listener is encouraged to ask, "Have you told that person?"

Often the answer is "no," so the employee is coached to deliver the compliment directly rather than gossiping (albeit in a good way) behind someone's back. At first it was awkward, but when the recipients lit up and people started feeling great about themselves, the practice caught on.

We could help change the culture in our workplaces by reminding people that a compliment is a gift of words.

myth

Stress and Fear are motivators

Most professionals are subject to stress for various reasons and often those stresses lead to fears about job security or performance. Unfortunately, some employers think they should exploit these anxieties as a motivational tool.

In fact stress and fear are deterrents for many people and because job stability is so uncertain these days, an increased number of workers are scared and insecure a good deal of the time anyway, which is most certainly not a good motivator for anyone!

Even if jobs are not at risk, you would think that leaders would have figured out that neither stress nor fear is especially successful at encouraging people to be more productive over the long term.

Story

Sales departments have a habit of constantly increasing sales expectations or expanding territories for those who meet their goals. At the end of the month, they often get the letter: "Congratulations. You were one of our top sellers this month. We assume you'll do even better next month." No matter what they do, or how well they perform, their stress is not reduced.

When we asked for his rationale for using this tactic a sales manager said, "Upping the ante is our motivational tool!"

It may work for some people, but not most. To never be quite good enough is analogous to running home to excitedly tell your parents that you got a 99 on your Biology test and them asking, "Which one did you get wrong?"

Even though a sales manager had himself worked under the same stressful model for years, he took a deep breath and decided to try encouraging his own sales team with more positive motivators. In less than 3 months, they reported being less stressed and more enthusiastic, both of which resulted in higher numbers.

myth

Programs such as
"Employee Of The Month" are motivating

Not if you're part of the group that doesn't ever receive the accolade.

The reason that reward and punishment are so closely tied is that if you don't get rewarded for doing a good job, it must mean that you're substandard. The absence of a reward can therefore be experienced as a punishment. Really competitive people might get into it, but those who are less competitive won't even try, and those in the middle become used to being in the middle.

Story

Employee of the Month was an honor that had been around for years. The award was accompanied by a photo in the cafeteria, a gift certificate to a nearby restaurant, and an acknowledgment in the company's newsletter and on its web site. But the managers were puzzled by the fact that some people didn't want it and those that didn't get it weren't even trying to work toward the goal.

At an executive staff meeting, several supervisors began remembering and sharing childhood stories about how humiliating it was when the teacher praised them in the classroom because it separated them from the group. Other kids made fun of them and being on top felt no better than being on the bottom. Either way, they were not like the rest.

You'd think we'd get used to occasionally being singled out for some accomplishment, but not everyone does. Apparently being a winner can sometimes be as uncomfortable and upsetting as being a loser.

If such rewards are now part of your culture, and you decide to take them away for the reasons stated above, it's important that you explain why, and perhaps celebrating successes company-wide might fill the gap.

myth

"Difficult Individuals" know how to straighten up and behave better, so they should!

People usually do what they do because they don't know how to do it any other way. I can assure you that they don't wake up in the morning saying, "With luck today nobody will like me" or "I think I'll make everybody mad by screwing up."

If employees need increased computer proficiency, we train them, and if they lack technical expertise, we give it to them, so how is it that we assume everyone has traditional and acceptable social behavior and never needs any coaching?

Story

One department boasted that they were comprised of the best and the brightest. However, one of their most skilled members was extremely negative. Much to their surprise one day he said, "I don't know why you have so much trouble with me. I'm the most positive person in my family!"

"My extended family has dinner together every Sunday because no one else wants to be with us. The conversation is mostly about the turkey not being done, the vegetables tasting terrible, and the fact that it's raining and we'll probably be in car accidents on the way home. I'm a whole lot more positive than that."

They finally decided to use him in the best sense of the word. When addressing pros and cons of a project, who better to be in charge of the cons than the negative person? The woman who kept looking at her watch became the timekeeper. The man who constantly doodled wrote on the board. There was a place for everyone.

Instead of trying to change people, they found a way to turn annoying habits into assets. Lightening up made a huge difference and when the environment became more supportive, they became less focused on what used to drive them crazy.

myth

Merit Pay is a great motivator

If everyone is getting a fair wage for doing a good job, then why have a merit pay program? Separately rewarding people "for a job well done" implies that whoever is not getting a bonus is underperforming.

I am convinced that merit pay reduces motivation, lowers productivity, and creates a toxic atmosphere for many. It also increases divisiveness and hurts teamwork.

If some team members get bonuses, those who don't will feel undervalued or like they're underperformers, employees will be in competition with one another, and performance and productivity will eventually decline.

Story

Arguing the above on a panel, I asked the person who disagreed with me most if he wanted his employees to do well only because they wanted a raise. "What if the economy suffers and you can't give raises?" I asked. "What will be their motivation to perform at high levels?"

My fellow panel member and some of the audience argued that I was casting doubt on a "sacred cow." Merit pay has been the carrot at the end of the workplace stick for a long time.

The only response I could think of was "Does that make it right or useful?"

myth

Employees care most about money

Everyone assumes that there is nothing more important than a good salary, but employees tell us that other things are just as important: having challenging work, the authority to accompany responsibilities, opportunities for growth, and the ability to provide valuable input.

Of course money is important, but how do you explain the numbers of people who turn down jobs with higher pay?

Story

A small company could not offer salaries competitive with the larger corporations in the area, yet they lost very few employees. The owner was surprised when one day the CEO from one of his major competitors invited him to lunch to find out why he couldn't lure employees away from the small shop even though he was offering higher wages.

The smaller firm's owner left laughing because he was sure that the CEO thought he was hiding something when he said, "We're just nicer to our people and we let them know how much we value them."

It really wasn't much more complicated than that, but the fact that the corporate CEO was convinced that his counterpart had some secret retention package spoke volumes.

myth

Exit interviews don't do much good

They don't if you don't care to learn why someone is leaving, what that person's experience has been, what observations and knowledge s/he can share about the work environment, and how the organization can be improved. The other benefit to having a meeting with the exiting employee is that s/he may leave with a much better feeling and be more likely to talk positively about your organization.

The challenge is to listen carefully and not interrupt or become defensive. This is an information gathering exercise - not an opportunity to talk the employee out of his or her perceptions.

Story

The Company numbered 350 employees and had never instituted exit interviews. In fact, supervisors often felt rejected when someone chose to leave so they adopted a "we don't care" attitude.

A new Vice President fought to include exit interviews and was willing to conduct them. She told employees she would only share generalities and whatever was said would not affect future references. Even she was surprised at the candor that emerged (a tribute to her non-judgmental approach, I'm sure), and she soon gathered information to which no one had been privy.

As a result of the interviews, the company has improved several systems, greatly enhanced their new employee orientation, fixed some small and a few major glitches in their process, and instituted supervisory training that has been received positively and with relief.

As one supervisor said, "They would promote us and then throw us into circumstances beyond our expertise. As a result of the training, we now have more skills and we meet regularly to provide peer supervision."

myth

Performance evaluations should be delivered only by supervisors for their direct reports, i.e. top down

Who knows better how you supervise than the people you supervise? They're often more knowledgeable than your boss. Despite it being common practice, the idea that performance evaluations should only be issued from top down doesn't make intuitive sense.

360 Degree Performance Evaluations include feedback from people surrounding an employee: direct and indirect reports, peers, his or her own supervisors, and perhaps customers, clients, and vendors, if the employee wishes. Richness is enhanced when it also includes a self-assessment.

Story

A company decided to implement a 360. They had the good sense to train everyone on how to give feedback so that it was developmental and not punitive. They also chose an online version that allowed certain specifics to go only to the person receiving the evaluation. That decision was made after employees said they wanted to provide honest feedback, but didn't want to get the person in trouble or skew his or her supervisor's perception.

It was a difficult transition, especially for those at the top because they weren't used to getting responses from employees farther down the line. However, they thought that the new process should begin with them so that they could provide a model of acceptance.

It became part of their culture within two years and many voiced that they couldn't imagine why they hadn't done it earlier. It has influenced their training programs, clarified problems, and enhanced communication at all levels.

myth

Departmental performance evaluations should be forced into a bell curve

Ahhhhhhh! (Was that not articulate enough?) In my opinion, it's unconscionable to artificially create a bell curve. I felt the same way in academic settings when the curve was forced rather than simply a graph of the range in which student grades fell.

Bell curves can be a result, but to manipulate an assessment to make sure there are outliers on both ends of the continuum is decidedly unfair and ethically suspect. At the very least, it is discriminatory.

People should not be in competition with each other. They are doing a good job or they're not, and either one should have little to do with their colleagues' performance.

Story

There wasn't enough money to give everyone a raise, so the administrators decided to force department heads to place some employees below the expected standards. The push back was dramatic. "But what if it's not true?" they asked. "What if I don't have any under-performing workers?" The answer was shocking. "You'll just have to find reasons that they belong there."

One supervisor quit and the others were disgruntled and felt guilty because they were lying. Over time, several of their best supervisors left because they could not bring themselves to manipulate the professional lives of the people who worked so hard for them.

They suggested that everyone would rather have smaller raises than see their workmates categorized unfairly.

myth

1-5 is a good range for performance evaluation rankings

It's too tempting to default to 3. Rankings aren't worthwhile unless accompanied by written explanations and even less helpful if they reflect a default position. If you must have numerical rankings, consider 1-4 so the person doing it has to really think about where the employee belongs. If comments are required, and they absolutely should be, the rationale for the chosen number will be even more important.

Story

A large corporation decided to assess their assessments. They first documented where employees fell on the continuum. It became immediately clear that the extremely high number of "3s" could not simply be a result of the bell curve.

Bringing managers and department heads together helped. During an open and honest dialogue, everyone admitted that it was too agonizing to figure out what rankings to use - especially since raises were tied to the outcome - so they often just put 3. They thought it would be harder to criticize because as one man said, "How can you argue with average?"

They decided to forget the rankings (a major step) and use only narratives. They trained everyone how to write them and what criteria to use. It was a new kind of agony but most (not all) agree that the performance evaluations are now much more meaningful and helpful.

myth

Everyone wants to be successful

Definitions of success are so varied that the term is not always a meaningful measure. For instance, the doctor who leaves a lucrative practice in New York City to move to Vermont where he or she will earn less but be able to spend more time with family, is not running from success but redefining it.

However, not everyone who turns down the chance to be "more successful" is redefining it. I wrote my Ph.D. dissertation on the Fear of Success (often referred to as Success Sabotage or Success Avoidance), so I can also assure you that some would truly like the promotion or opportunity, but may sabotage his or her chances.

For that person, it may be that familiarity is more comfortable than taking on a new identity and/or self-perception. Even self-described failures will say, "The upside is that I know how to be me."

Story

The most talented man in the company talked about wanting promotions but always found some excuse to refuse them when they were offered. When a mentorship program was put into place, his mentor asked him why he kept saying no. After several sessions, he said, "There will be no end to their expectations; I'll have less freedom to make mistakes; I don't want to be my peer's supervisor; I'm not used to having power; I'll lose friends; I'm uncomfortable with the unknown; and being a boss doesn't fit my self-image."

The supervisor asked, "How can we help?" and was tempted to say, "I know you can do it!" but had the good sense to wait patiently for an answer because he realized the importance of the employee believing that he was capable. With the promise that he'd get all the help he needed, he finally accepted the promotion and became a successful leader, though he still seeks guidance from time to time.

myth

There is no need for supervisors to be in agreement about performance evaluation rankings

Performance Evaluations usually include rankings on a scale from unsatisfactory, to meeting expectations, to excellent. Too often there's not agreement about what those rankings represent. Each supervisor often decides for him or herself.

When meeting with those who conduct performance evaluations, there is usually a healthy debate. "I never give 5's because there's always room for improvement." Another says, "I always give some 5's because it's motivating." As the discussion continues, there's further dialogue about what each ranking category means and the criteria for assigning a particular rank.

If this were a class, the conversation would be welcomed, but if the supervisors are all part of the same organization, it suggests different interpretations and evaluative methods, which could be a major problem.

Story

An employee sued the company for wrongful termination because his previous supervisor had given him fairly high rankings, but his new supervisor said that he fell below the acceptable standard. His production levels were the same for both.

Last I knew the suit was still pending, but since then the company has offered extensive training in which they've included an activity that asks all supervisors to agree on what each ranking number means, the criteria for meeting it, and practice in how to write the accompanying narratives.

There are still some differences, but they've been minimized.

myth

Evaluations should summarize performance over the past year

Performance Evaluations are usually designed to look at the year gone by, but I think that should be re-examined. Only 25% of PE's should be about the past 12 months, 15% should be about the present, and a full 65% should focus on the future. The past and present should inform the future. You want your employees thinking ahead, not lamenting the past.

Story

It was just by chance that the President of the company came across the above notion. It seemed weird to him so he wondered why he kept thinking about it. Maybe it wasn't so strange, he thought, and decided to bring it up at the annual leadership retreat.

As the conversation evolved, his colleagues admitted that the past is behind us. "There is nothing we can do about it, but we can influence the future."

They designed a new evaluation form and hosted 3 meetings to explain it to all the employees. They said that from now on, the bulk of the evaluation sessions would be devoted to identifying the help that people needed to improve, what training would be required, and what barriers existed that kept people from performing well and reaching their goals.

This new approach took a fair amount of retraining for both the supervisors and the staff.

myth

Yearly performance evaluation meetings are the time to let people know how they're doing

That's too late. There should not be any surprises on performance evaluations. If there are, it means that the employee hasn't been informed about his or her performance in a timely fashion. The annual review (I wish it were more often) is a time to corroborate and document what has already been communicated and it's an opportunity to explore the future.

Story

Because most of the supervisors disliked doing performance evaluations, they waited as long as they could and delivered them only when forced by HR. The only thing that many of them avoided more was giving meaningful feedback on a regular basis.

No wonder they didn't look forward to the annual review. Who wouldn't anticipate the meeting with trepidation when it was the only designated time to tell employees how and when they were not meeting expectations?

It was a huge leap for the company to announce that the yearly performance evaluation would be a time to summarize what the employee had already been told throughout the year. In other words, no surprises!

It took at least two rounds to make this happen and now it's common procedure. When asked what they like most about the new format, both employees and supervisors report that no one comes in nervous and the conversations are much more productive.

Communication
Conflict

myth

If I don't say it perfectly the first time I've lost my chance

If perfection were the goal, most of us would be stymied and say very little. Still, we're so intent on getting it right at the outset that we often labor under the misconception that we can't self-correct.

It's okay to try again - and again. Human relations are about process, not product. We can make other attempts. We can go back and say, "Our last conversation didn't go well. Can we try it again?" or ask "What could I have done differently?"

Story

So often people leave a conversation saying, "I should have said this. I should have said that." It's what I call "shoulding on ourselves."

One high powered executive told me that when he comes in the next day and says, "You know, I've been going over what happened at the meeting yesterday and thought we should have another conversation," employees are astounded that he put in any time thinking about it and them. What people hear is, "Wow, he thought about us overnight. He must really care!"

myth

It's important not to share unsettling information prematurely

The "don't tell the kids" approach doesn't work with kids, so why would it work with adults? If parents are struggling, the children know that something's wrong, and in the absence of clear information, their imaginations run wild. Like grown ups, their fantasies are often worse than reality.

We hire adults: people who are raising their families, paying their rent or mortgages, and functioning in the world that reflects their age and stage in life. Yet in the workplace, they are often treated like children.

When secrets are kept from employees, suspicion reins, distrust prevails, and energy is directed toward wondering what is going on instead of being focused on the work required. People are left with the fear of the unknown.

Story

A major downsizing was announced, and then nothing was said about it for 3 months. Employees were beside themselves and rumors were rampant.

When I asked why he hadn't told his employees anything the CEO said "I don't know anything." I said, "Well at least tell them that much because they think you know something and are keeping it to yourself." I suggested that even if he had no further information, he should keep them apprised throughout the day so they might have some relief from worry, at least for a few hours.

The CEO was surprised to learn that even the updates that lacked much substance calmed his employees. It turned out that something was better than nothing because then everyone knew that when there was information to share, they would hear it in a timely fashion. In the meantime, they didn't have to spend needless energy second guessing.

myth

People should only be given information on a need-to-know basis

Why limit what is shared? Who decides what anyone needs to know? Can't they be trusted with information? Aren't they smart enough to assimilate it? Aren't they revered enough to be let in on what's going on?

If you truly think that your employees aren't trustworthy, smart, or important, perhaps they shouldn't be working for you. And if you're worried about overloading them with information, let them tell you when it's enough or invite them to ask for more clarification if they need it.

Story

The Vice President of HR decided to ask a cross-section of employees what kinds of information they would like on an ongoing basis. They responded immediately with the questions they wanted answered.

- How secure is the company and will you tell us if that changes?
- Am I meeting expectations?
- How can I improve, and will you provide the resources to help me?
- Are there opportunities to advance and how do I do that?
- If expectations change, will you tell us?
- How is my performance being evaluated?
- Will you keep us apprised of changes and how they might affect us?

It was clear that employees weren't asking for much and what they did wish to know was perfectly reasonable. The secretiveness that had been the norm had caused enormous anxiety and distrust, but once information was readily shared - including the ever-changing financial situation - trust began to build, performance improved, and people appeared more relaxed.

myth

Staff meetings should be cancelled during busy times

The opposite is true. We should increase communication when work life is stressful. The time taken to communicate will reduce confusion, fear, and misunderstanding.

It's tempting to eliminate staff meetings when deadlines loom and stress levels are high, and you'll definitely get a lot of support from employees if you do. In the long run, however, they'll be much more upset about the lack of communication and connectedness.

Story

Stress was high in a manufacturing plant because of an unprecedented number of orders for the product, so they bought time by eliminating staff meetings.

Two weeks into the craziness, the managers noticed that people were congregating much more often around the coffee pot, in the hallways, and in the parking lot. They weren't wasting time; they were filling the need to communicate with the partial information they could feed one another.

Unfortunately, since the people with most of the information were not involved, the conversations revolved around rumors and possibilities.

Luckily, those in charge got the message and reinstated the needed gatherings.

myth

Little things aren't worth talking about

True if you also don't care about the big things! Seemingly small, even frivolous issues often represent something much bigger and are usually associated with status, fairness, and trust.

Consider the little things people complain about: paper not being replaced in the copier, temperature in the workplace, parking availability, and dirty dishes in the sink. Once you start talking about the complaints, note how quickly the discussion moves to respect, consideration, status differential, and responsibility.

Story

I once worked in an office where there were constant complaints about the coffee pot. It was assumed that women, not men, should make sure there was coffee all day long and it was expected that the support staff should clean up even though they were busier than the professional staff at the end of the day.

One insightful employee finally observed that this same pattern of behavior was going on with projects: work was not being apportioned fairly and not everyone was pulling their fair share of the weight.

Because it was safer to discuss the coffee pot than projects, they started with that discussion first, which then led easily into the larger discussion of project management.

myth

Email is the perfect way to communicate

People read email in the mood they're in and not necessarily in the mood it was created, which is why this fabulous technological invention has caused enormous communication problems.

Try saying something several different ways and note that depending on your tone of voice, you may be delivering very different messages. Tone is lost in the written word so the reader overlays how s/he thinks the message was meant to be delivered.

Story

I worked with a company where people complained that their emails were often taken the wrong way. They said things like "Colleagues thought I was mad and I wasn't" or "I was mad and no one got it."

They developed a new policy that I now share with others. If there is tension in emails, it isn't likely to improve with subsequent messages, so now only 2 tense exchanges are allowed.

After that, the writers have to either meet in person or talk on the phone if they're not in close proximity. They can then check out if they interpreted the message correctly. If the answer is yes, the discussion or argument can continue.

myth

Talking and writing
are our primary modes of communication

In fact much of our communication takes place through our body language – raising our eyebrows, smiling or frowning, squinting our eyes, pursing our lips, shaking and nodding our heads, moving our arms, turning away, and a myriad of other gestures that deliver messages that may or may not be interpreted correctly, which means you're communicating with your body whether you like it or not!

Here is the more disconcerting part: everyone else knows more about your body language than you know about your own because you can't see yourself. People report that they're shocked when they watch themselves in a video because their movements seem foreign.

The good news is that there is a way to deliver accurate messages. If what you're saying matches what you're thinking your body language will be more congruent.

Story

I'm not suggesting that you think about your body language. Actually, that would be difficult because you don't know what it looks like. Here is what happens if you try.

I choreograph for a local theater company and years ago a woman in the cast was concerned. She had the dance steps down but she couldn't figure out what to do with her arms. So I said: "It's quite simple. You do the same thing with your arms that you do when you walk."

Her eyes glazed over. She had never thought about what she did when she walked. To this day - years later - she freezes in place when she sees me, unable to walk and swing her arms correctly in my presence. I think to myself "Great! She came in unable to dance and went out unable to walk!"

myth

What we say is all that matters

Mere stance and proximity can be unsettling, especially if there is a power differential. The boss standing over the shoulder of the employee, the CEO sitting behind a big desk in a slightly higher chair than his or her visitors, or a person in power entering someone's personal space: all these examples work to exaggerate the relative importance of the people engaged in the interchange.

Story

There is a difference in interaction when both parties are sitting or standing rather than one towering over the other. When cultural differences around personal space are respected, conversations are much improved. When the boss comes out from behind the desk and sits across from people - without barriers - s/he is bound to encourage a more fruitful dialogue.

There are also times when stature unfairly plays a role. I have a friend who is a very sweet guy but quite tall and big. Sadly, he has found that he has to stand farther away from people than most because he's perceived as threatening just because of his physical characteristics. He has learned to talk more softly for the same reason.

It's not fair, of course, because it's a form of stereotyping. His response is, "Nevertheless, I do whatever makes it easier for both the other person and me. The goal is to get my point across. If my stature is going to interfere with that, then I make accommodations."

myth

Making eye contact is always important

Sometimes eye contact can be perceived as a challenge and puts people on the defensive. Despite conventional wisdom, eye contact is not always a good way to draw out information. Turning ever so slightly when standing or sitting next to a person, especially when the conversation is beginning to feel adversarial, delivers the message that "We're in this together" and heading in the same direction.

It's not by chance that people disclose more when they're walking together or that kids tell parents more in the car than they do around the dinner table. Strangers tell you more on a plane or a bus than you ever want to know. It feels like you're going in the same direction - you're on the same side.

Story

A group of public employees were charged with helping citizens fill out forms at the counter. The customers were often distressed and unhappy about their situations and confused about how to proceed.

The staff tried turning slightly as they explained what was needed and found that it was like magic. People calmed down and felt allied with the person serving them.

myth

Conversations can be taken at face value

It's amazing that we get along as well as we do. To every conversation we bring the influence of our childhood experience, the neighborhood where we were raised, historical events we've witnessed, what has happened that day, how we're feeling physically, and our temperaments and personalities.

We are the sum total of our experience which is why others can't know us as well as we know ourselves. At the risk of treading into psychobabble, consider all the times we engage in transference and projection by responding to colleagues as though they are people from our past or by projecting our own insecurities on to them.

Story

Life was not easy at a dynamic PR firm. It was baffling because the work was exciting and the talent in the group extraordinary. They blamed the constant tension on the fact that they were sensitive, creative people always dealing with looming deadlines. It turned out that the built-in chaos served to mask the real issues.

At an off-site retreat, the facilitator's first suggestion was that each person write down, and save for later, how each felt about their colleagues.

Throughout the 3 days, they began to realize how many of their responses to one another were based on assumptions, faulty information, and stylistic differences. At the end, they were asked to again write down how they felt about their co-workers.

In many instances, there was no comparison to their original list. It was as though they were talking about two different people. They left stunned, humbled, much more connected, and committed to checking out the truth before jumping to conclusions.

It proves the adage that "assumptions are guesses that we begin to believe."

myth

If there are different accounts about the same event, somebody's not telling the truth

Leaders need to know what happened, who is responsible, how did we get that outcome, or what went wrong and they rely on their employees to explain.

Because there are often many variables affecting people's interpretations of an event or exchange, no one should be surprised when hearing differing views about the same experience.

Getting to the factual truth without embarrassing or negatively judging people should be the goal. Life is about perception, so make sure to implement procedures that ask for and receive clarification before acting on information.

Story

A mugging was staged at a conference. The so-called victim was removed and the so-called police were brought in to question the witnesses.

The descriptions of the perpetrator crossed gender and racial lines, and the descriptions of height ranged from 5'2" to over 6' tall.

The reliability of witnesses is questionable. In fact, police will often report that they'll have 5 different witnesses at an accident, reporting 5 different stories, and nobody is lying. Each person is convinced that his/her report is true.

myth

When someone is emotional responding logically is helpful

Not unless you also think talking Spanish to French-speaking people is effective. We need to speak the same language.

Connecting with people is easiest when you are where they are. If they're expressing their emotions, you need to be open to listening. The good news is that you don't have to understand their emotion, nor do you have to share it. You just need to acknowledge that you appreciate what they're experiencing.

When people are distressed, they feel disconnected. When we respond with logic, we push them even farther away. They just want to know that somebody "gets it." Once that connection is made, they're much more apt to say, "Okay, what should I do about it?" At that point you can share logical suggestions.

Story

Perhaps this is your scenario. You've had an awful day. You're frustrated, angry, depressed, and overwhelmed. At the end of the day, you say to someone who cares about you, "I've had a terrible day. I'm frustrated, angry, depressed, and overwhelmed." Trying to fix it, your friend says "Well if you had done this, this, and this, you would have had a better day."

Do you think you'd say, "Thanks I feel better?" Most likely not. You'd probably feel even worse. When you started the conversation, you had just one problem. Now you feel like an idiot because you clearly didn't know what to do.

Again, feelings aren't right or wrong. They just are.

myth

"Why" questions elicit a thoughtful response

In American culture, "Why?" is often received as an accusation, not as a question. "Why did you say that?" "Why were you late?" "Why didn't you hand in the report on time?"

The person asking the question really meant "I don't like what you said." "I'm upset that you're late." "You were remiss not handing in the report on time," which is why the response is usually defensive or "I don't know."

There is a better way to ask such questions: "Can you explain what you meant?" "Will you share the reason it's hard to get here on time?" "Tell me more about how the report is coming and what might be holding it up." You're much more apt to get an accurate explanation.

Story

We ask 4 years olds why they spilled milk on the floor. What would you consider a reasonable answer? "I hated the tile?" "I wanted to make you mad?" "It was fun?" Even little kids know that we're leveling an accusation and that it's not an open question.

Develop your own story. Try going through a day not asking "Why?" Substitute What, When, How, and Tell Me More. It's not easy, but it will be fascinating to note the differences in the responses you receive.

myth

"You" messages are effective

"You" messages are too often received as accusatory and pushy, especially when they're accompanied by pointing. It puts people on the defensive or pushes them up against an imaginary wall where they can only fight back or cower.

"I" messages, on the other hand, have a softer effect and the speaker is taking some of the responsibility for the interaction.

Story

Consider the difference between "You're offensive," and "When you do that, I'm offended." The first is accusatory and usually results in an argument that could go on forever. The latter doesn't accuse so much as inform the speaker that his or her actions are difficult for the receiver.

Another example: "You're yelling," versus "When you talk loudly, I shut down and don't hear half of what you're saying." I'm not judging you for talking loudly; what I'm saying is that when you do, I don't hear you. I'm taking responsibility for my own reaction and the person can decide whether it's more important to make me uncomfortable or attempt a different approach.

myth

Being judgmental inevitably leads to discrimination

Worse than having judgments is being judgmental and not acknowledging it to ourselves. We're not proud of our prejudices, so owning up to them is difficult, but consider the following.

Prejudice is generalizing about a group, and discrimination is acting on it. If we don't want to discriminate, then we have to acknowledge that we have the prejudice. It's not easy because it's often embarrassing and the pressure is on because it's ours to solve.

Story

A new Executive Director shared his experience. He was the son of Holocaust survivors and very sensitive to the dangers of prejudice and discrimination. He asked that his executive team take part in an exercise that honestly assessed where their prejudices resided. He agreed to do the same. They learned that the following categories were absolutely true for them.

Where the prejudice was intentional, they purposely discriminated, i.e. they didn't include employees under thirty in the decision-making process.

Where it was covert, they realized that many of their expressions were sexist and ageist, especially regarding people over 60.

A few on the leadership team engaged in intentional discrimination of a racist nature that they tried to hide. They, too, were embarrassed to even admit to themselves that they had secretly blocked employees of color from being promoted.

The biggest challenge was the unintentional and well-hidden. They were unaware of those prejudices and how those who were discriminated against felt marginalized. Because their willingness to engage in self-assessment was very impressive, employees increasingly felt it was safe to point out discriminatory behavior rather than wait for it to be acknowledged.

myth

Political Correctness
is an unnecessary annoyance

The requirement to be politically correct reminds us of our stereotypes and biases. It's like spell-check.

Story

I understand why political correctness can be burdensome, but here's what convinced me of its importance. A few years ago I decided to have my bangs cut at the small hair salon in the hotel where I was delivering a speech the next day.

When I had been there the year before, I remembered that the stylist used to have a larger salon and asked him if he liked this better. "Oh yes" he said. "You wouldn't believe who used to come to my old shop." He then berated one ethnic, racial, and religious group after another! I don't know what group he belonged to because I don't think there were any left.

I was shocked! Here I was a stranger, and he didn't even wonder whether he might be insulting me! He eventually did, so I summoned the courage I was surprised I needed and said, "I would have been just as offended even if I didn't belong to the last group you disparaged." He was as surprised by my reaction as I was appalled by his rhetoric.

It was the moment I realized I'd rather have people insincerely politically correct than sincerely discriminatory so we can get through our lives with less distress.

myth

In order to appear competent
you must have an answer ready
as soon as the other person stops speaking

This requires preparing a response while someone is still talking, which is just a step away from speaking while they're talking.

If you even begin thinking about what to say, you clearly can't be listening.

Story

A caring supervisor called in his management staff and asked a provocative question. "I have weekly meetings just to hear your concerns, but I often get the message that I'm not listening. Can you tell me what's going on?"

His direct reports told him that they appreciated his willingness to meet with them but that he was so intent on helping he sometimes offered answers before they were finished delivering information. Many times his answers were not even related to the questions they wanted to address.

Though he acknowledged it was going to require a major adjustment in his communication style, he agreed to try his best to be focused on what they were saying or asking, not on forming a response. It meant changing a lifetime pattern, but his willingness to try created a lot of good will.

myth

Assertiveness is a more palatable way to be aggressive

No, it's not, because the intent behind aggressiveness is to dominate in order to get one's own way at the expense of others, while assertiveness allows people to straightforwardly express their needs and feelings while still respecting other people's rights.

Story

At lunch, non-smoking employees went outside to get some air, but smokers lit up near them which was extremely bothersome.

The aggressive approach would be "Put out the cigarettes! You're polluting the air for all of us!"

The non-assertive approach - when people deny their needs and give up their rights - would be to do nothing and suffer.

The more effective, assertive approach which would respect everyone's rights would be: "We're having trouble breathing the second hand smoke and you're having trouble taking a break without smoking. Can we figure out a solution that works for both of us?"

myth

It's best to deliver bad news on a Friday or before a holiday break

Honest managers will admit that it's tempting to fire people, down-size, or deliver a doom & gloom report late Friday afternoon or before a holiday so that the leadership team doesn't have to deal with any emotional reactions. All sorts of other reasons are given, but frankly it's a self-protective move.

If the message must be delivered, choose a Tuesday or Wednesday when employees have access to people who can answer the inevitable questions they forgot to ask in the disturbing meeting.

Story

This guy had to be let go. He was disruptive, unproductive, and not suited for the job. At 4:00 PM on Friday afternoon, he was urged to clean off his desk and not talk to anyone before leaving.

Not surprisingly, after his wife began to recover from the devastating news, she asked, "Will we have health insurance?" "Will you get your unused vacation and sick pay?" "Will your supervisor write you a reference letter?"

Because it was now the weekend, HR was unavailable and there was no one else to provide answers to questions affecting the rest of their lives, so the family spiraled downward.

By the time Monday rolled around, the former employee was furious and instead of calling the office for answers he contacted his lawyer about filing a lawsuit for unfair termination.

myth

Conflict is inherently negative and always about the issue

Conflict is not necessarily negative and it's not usually about the issue. It results from the way the conversation is handled. The next time you witness an altercation, notice how quickly it moves from the topic to "You're not listening to me" or "You always talk to me like that!"

Story

I met a woman who described her 30-year business partnership as nothing short of a longevity miracle since she and her partner had two totally different conflict management styles.

She was brought up in a household that didn't allow conflict. If you were unhappy about something, you went into your room until you felt better. While on a business trip, her partner invited her to his extended family gathering.

She was shocked at the level of bickering and raised voices and said, "Apparently, this is a bad time." He replied, "What do you mean? That's how we say "hello." They fight all day about everything at the same level of intensity.

When he would become dramatic, she'd think "He's leaving." When she wouldn't fight with him, he'd think, "She's leaving. She must not like me any more."

What happened to them is what happens to most people, so unless we understand each other's stylistic differences, we can only assume the other person is feeling like we would feel if we acted that way.

It could be dead wrong.

myth

Personality conflicts are the main reason people argue with each other

Most workplace arguments are about role confusion or lack of clear process. "I thought you were doing that." "But that was my job." "You're not the boss of me." "I thought we were proceeding this way." "You're doing it wrong."

Once roles and processes are clarified, you'll be surprised at how much conflict disappears.

Story

The Company tripled in size. Good news, of course, because the product was successful. Everyone felt much more secure than they had when they were deemed a "start up," so they now had every reason to be in a constant state of celebration.

The ensuing conflicts and snide comments made behind people's backs were completely unexpected, and as time went on people felt increasingly unsafe and some began to describe the workplace as toxic.

It was agreed that a conversation was needed to figure out how they had gone from a cheerful, comfortable workplace to one that was no longer tolerable. What could possibly have gone wrong?

During the first two years everyone pitched in to do everything to get the company off the ground, but they had grown out of that stage and hadn't realized it, so there was a great deal of confusion about who was supposed to do what and how things were supposed to get done. In one case, a rather simple task turned out to have three different approaches.

A facilitated team building session helped establish a procedure for clarifying roles and responsibilities. It is now something they do whenever there is a change in the size of the company.

myth

It's only the tension between people that causes conflict

It is tempting to blame conflict on individuals, but it may well be a systemic issue. There's an excellent chance that what is going on in the larger organization and in society is impacting the employees, causing tension, and resulting in strained relationships.

It's not surprising that reports of conflict increase during recessions, restructuring efforts, budget crises, and leadership changes.

Story

I often get calls reporting that "Our employees used to get along great and now they're arguing all the time." I ask, "Is there anything going on systemically in the larger organization that's different?" Often the answer is "Yes."

Because it's not easy or particularly smart to argue with the boss, people tend to take their frustrations and concerns out on each other. Also, be aware that the reason for annoyance with one's colleagues may not be conscious. The old saying, "We take it out on those closest to us," can also be true at work.

myth

When employees are having issues with one another, it's best to speak with them separately to find out what's going on

When I facilitate conflict in organizations, I make it a point not to speak with individuals before meeting with the group because it means I then have to hold secrets and be careful about what I share.

If a tone is set by the facilitator that ensures safety and doesn't tolerate scapegoating, the discomfort of bringing up issues in the group lasts for about 15 minutes, after which the conversation is usually vibrant and substantive. People figure out that it's to everyone's advantage to be supportive of one another and disagreements are more easily resolved.

Story

This should be called "No Win." Three employees were at odds and their increasing tension and conflict came to the attention of their supervisor. Following the usual path, the boss decided to meet with each person separately to find out each individual's take on the problem.

Everyone's stories made sense from their personal perspectives, so now the supervisor was stuck with no way to objectively assess who was right or what should be done to help everyone see different viewpoints. Nothing changed.

Had they all met together with good facilitation from the outset, they would have realized that it wasn't a matter of right and wrong, but more about appreciating each other's points of view. They may not have agreed with one another's conclusions, but they would have understood what fueled them and had a better chance of resolving their discord.

myth

Compromise and loss are synonymous

The act of compromising is often misconstrued. True compromise is win/win, not win/lose and certainly not lose/lose, and just because it's called a compromise doesn't mean it is.

Story

If we get to the movies early enough, I almost always see people arguing about which one to see. "We're going to this movie." "No, we're going to that movie." So it's this movie/that movie all the way across the parking lot. They get to the box office and buy tickets for a 3rd movie neither of them wants to see and think they've compromised because they're both equally miserable.

A true compromise would be: "We'll go to your movie tonight and mine tomorrow night." Or "You go to yours and I'll go to mine and we'll meet for coffee afterwards." (If it happens every weekend, maybe they should go to the movies with someone different, which is probably why they're not talking about it.)

What examples are there from your own organization where people either voted or nodded in agreement, yet were unhappy with the result? Negotiating a win/win does take more time, but not nearly as much time as dealing with the disappointing aftermath.

myth

"Avoiding" and "verbally attacking" are acceptable responses in conflictual situations

Attacking doesn't work at all because the other person can only respond in one of 3 ways: run away (either physically or psychologically), succumb by "giving in," or attack back.

In day-to-day life, though avoidance may work in the short run, it is not usually effective in the long run.

None of these leads to reasonable work or personal relationships.

Story

Because there was so much tension around whether the company would continue to be viable, everyone was on edge and those at the top had little patience for the conflict that continually erupted. Several supervisors acted like the VP in charge of Operations: when confronted with conflict, he either didn't respond or he lashed out at the "offenders."

When avoidance was in play, people felt discounted and ignored. When he attacked, strong people yelled back, those who were less secure "disappeared" and hid, and most just gave in without sharing the necessary information.

After an effective communication workshop, they identified their personal styles and took the opportunity to practice more effective conflict resolution skills. The fact that they experienced the workshop together resulted in a major cultural shift. It wasn't an overnight transition, but even slow progress was appreciated.

myth

Trust me

When it comes to trust, there is no substitute for time. It's rarely possible to trust someone immediately or wholly. In some cases, it's not even safe to do so. We are creatures designed to self-protect and when safety is threatened it takes a long time to rebuild whatever trust had been gained.

Story

A former CEO was fired for being duplicitous and left a wake of hurt behind. When his replacement came in, she understood that it would be a long rebuilding process. Fortunately, she was willing to wait and prove herself, not just once, but over and over again. People began coming around.

Then they stopped.

They were afraid this new CEO might also leave which would make the workplace unsafe again, so to protect themselves from this potential hurt, they were reluctant to embrace her.

Much to their credit, the entire team eventually worked their way through the impasse and decided that enjoying the improved environment was worth the possible risk of it being temporary.

myth

Informing people of your communication and conflict resolution styles gives you the freedom to be you

There is a difference between an excuse and an explanation. If you say, "This is who I am and you just have to live with it because I'm not going to change," is an excuse for your uncompromising behavior. If you truly want a better relationship with your employees, it's better to explain your style by saying "This is who I am and this is how I communicate." Then invite the other person to share his/her style which leads to negotiation and working out a true compromise.

By the way, it's best to have that conversation when the difficult interaction isn't taking place, and even better to have it while on a walk or over a cup of coffee.

Story

A well-qualified and industrious woman thought she was going to have to quit her job because her boss was very difficult when he was stressed. At her wit's end she confronted him and said, "When you blow up, I shut down and can't work, even when it has nothing to do with me!"

They agreed that he would try to control himself, but if he did have an episode, she would leave his office and do what she needed to do to feel better. They would talk about the incident later. It was a negotiated agreement to which they both committed and it worked.

Her leaving reminded him that his response was inappropriate. He found himself wanting to change and his explosive behavior diminished.

When he lapsed, she had permission to walk away.

Teaming
Group Dynamics

myth

Sports teams are great models for workplace teams

Sports teams are invested in beating each other, winning, and emerging triumphant. Is that how you want colleagues and departments to feel about one another?

It isn't that we can't learn from the sports experience. There are many examples of teams having the best talent in the world and losing, and others who have less talent taking home the honors. The difference is how highly they regard their teammates and how well they work together.

It's also important to clarify your definition of team. Departments? Sections? The entire organization?

Story

Being a sports enthusiast, the Sales Manager decided it would be great to have each sales group adopt the name of a major league baseball team. And it was fun for a while. The "Red Sox" and "Yankees" worked to beat one another. Other teams did the same. The competition fueled a frenzy of hard work.

However, customers started noticing that the company no longer appeared friendly. If they called one department, there was less enthusiasm for getting them to more appropriate staff in another section. Territoriality became the norm which hurt the customer as much as it hurt the employees.

Finally, the boss said, "We've created mortal enemies. Fun notwithstanding, it's not working." Now it's "Team Us" rather than "Team Us and Team Them."

myth

Internal competition increases productivity

Internal competition also encourages secretiveness, reluctance to share, stunted communication, and an undermining of teamwork, all of which get in the way of achieving organizational goals. Though it's tempting to try motivating workers by telling them that other shifts or departments are more productive, for many it has the opposite intended effect. People give up or give in, and collegial cordiality disappears.

Story

In a 24/7 factory, there was much shift-to-shift conflict. "They're leaving the place messy!" "No one on the previous shift cares about repairing the machines." "They have it easier than we do."

Top leadership agreed to allow a full day retreat with representatives from all 4 shifts. It was tense at the outset, but increasingly less so as they resolved a number of issues such as asking for overlap time so that the previous shift could update the oncoming workers about what to expect.

The best suggestions came from the floor employees, not the supervisors. My favorite was from a 23 year old guy who had only been working there a few months. He said, "The reason we're not nice to each other is that they have us pitted against one another. Instead of counting production at the end of each shift, how about if we count it from the middle of one to the middle of the next? Then, we'll want to make sure we've set up for the oncoming employees because we'll be in it together."

3 months later they reported that shift-to-shift conflict had virtually disappeared and no one missed the so-called "competitive spirit."

myth

Our only customers
are people who buy our products or services

The new philosophy challenges this narrow definition and recognizes that people inside an organization may also be "customers."

This philosophy has been called hokey, a fad, or just plain silly, but the rationale behind it has merit. Keep in mind that a company should be working to please the external customer as well as anyone within the organization to whom product or information is provided.

Story

Instituting the notion of "internal customers" was a lot harder than the administrative team thought. Pushback ranged from eye-rolling to out-and-out resistance, mostly because convention was being challenged: "They're not customers, they're colleagues"

At a full staff retreat, employees broke into small groups and were asked to list how they thought external customers should be treated. The company was very "customer friendly" so this was an easy list to generate.

They were then asked to cross off anything that didn't apply to "internal customers." Almost nothing was eliminated

The CEO ended the session: "I rest my case. Let's eat."

myth

Groups should coalesce right away

But they don't and for good reason.

Groups, large and small, go through predictable developmental stages. Just because they're called a team or have a departmental name does not mean they are a cohesive unit.

To become one, the members have to get to know one another and trust that they can share a diversity of opinions. They need to identify a culture and way of being, and all this usually happens before they can perform at the highest levels. Further, if just one person joins or leaves the group, they're back to the beginning. Not back to zero, but they are a new group that will inevitably go through the "forming" stage" again.

Story

A struggling department met to discuss their self-described dysfunction. The most articulate of the bunch said they couldn't function as a perfect unit because they seemed disconnected much of the time.

"Most of us have been here for years but several people have left for other jobs or retired, and we probably get at least 2 new people every few months. But essentially, we're the same group, so I don't know why we feel divided."

The group may be responsible for the same tasks, but any time there's a compositional change, it's a new group that must be acknowledged and re-formed.

myth

You shouldn't ask new hires for input until they've been there a while

New people have a wealth of information. They notice things the rest of the staff is used to, but they don't say anything because, well, they're new. By the time they feel comfortable enough to comment, they've adjusted to the norm and have long-forgotten their initial observations.

Story

A forward-looking non-profit meets with its newest hires a few weeks after they've arrived and asks them two pivotal questions. "What have you noticed?" and "What more could we have done to facilitate your orientation?"

Every comment and suggestion is carefully considered, and if it has any merit, it goes on the reassessment list. As a result, they've made a number of changes to procedures and processes that were no longer relevant or efficient.

Further, new employees feel like they've added value from the start.

myth

We'd be the perfect staff or department if it weren't for that one person

There may be an underlying motivation for allowing that "one person" to continue his or her behavior. The term "group collusion" implies that we let people act in certain ways because it serves us.

Remember the student who acted out in class? We loved that kid because it meant that we didn't have to do math for 10 minutes while the teacher dealt with the situation.

Allowing others to engage in behavior we say we don't like may be oddly functional. "If she's always arguing with the boss, and telling him what's wrong, then I don't have to do it." "If he's hard to be around, it makes it look like I'm easier to be around."

Story

Imagine you're on a staff where one person in the group complains a lot and monopolizes the conversation while everyone else seems easy to get along with and a pleasure to have in meetings.

Despite how it looks the complainer is serving the key role of articulating issues and problems so others don't have to do it.

It's important to recognize that everyone may be colluding to let him or her continue, so consider appreciating rather than criticizing that colleague for the beneficial role he or she is playing.

myth

Too much diversity
can be an impediment

Most of us say that we like diversity but we still want everyone to be just like us so we can move more smoothly and quickly.

Story

Minutes after starting a facilitation, I can usually identify the "big picture" people and the task-oriented "here and now" participants.

When the big picture people are talking, those who are detail-oriented are jumping out of their skins, waiting to fill in the task list. They want to know what to do when.

When we get to the details, those who see the big picture are often staring out the window or glazing over.

Together they're one perfect person. An effective and efficient organization needs people with different skills, different personalities, different ways to think about things, and different stress points.

myth

It's best if colleagues who work together have similar styles

Teams and departments are increasingly engaging in personality profile assessments. There are many instruments that accurately place people in categories describing their work and personal styles. If used correctly they help colleagues better understand, communicate, and empathize with one another.

Though people are often excited about working with others who share their style, they may be missing important perspectives and alternative approaches.

Story

After a departmental assessment revealed that almost everyone had similar styles, they were baffled. "If we're so similar, why aren't we better at coming up with good solutions and strategic directions?"

Similarity was the issue! There just wasn't enough diversity in the group to provide a total picture.

Though it felt good to be on the same page they couldn't turn it and often described themselves as stuck. The absence of diversity kept them from making progress.

On the next project they agreed to purposely invite colleagues from other departments with different approaches, and though it required patience and adjustment they were rewarded with more spirited discussions and the unique solutions that were missing from previous projects.

myth

Quiet people are not engaged

Shy individuals are often quiet so they won't be visible, not because they're uninvolved. If you want them to be engaged, you need to find the best way to elicit their contributions. For some, it may be written follow-up to a meeting. For others a one-to-one conversation and others may just need time to process.

Story

The new VP was very quiet at meetings. People thought she wasn't participating because it wasn't worth her time and everyone took it personally - until they all took a personality style assessment.

They discovered the VP was shy, and when they asked her why she hadn't told them, she said "Because I'm shy," so they settled on a process that worked for her: she would take notes, process the information, and then offer feedback to the group.

Most everyone agreed it was okay for other quiet people to explore alternatives for participating in a manner comfortable for them.

myth

Young people don't have a good work ethic

This is a stereotype every generation has about the one coming up.

Changing technology and different societal norms mean that attitudes about work are evolving all the time. Today young people may not be as deferential to authority, or they may want more of a work/life balance, and they may prefer communicating through technological means rather than face-to-face.

Succeeding generations will be different, so we might as well accept this constant evolution and find ways to adapt.

Story

At our son's college graduation, I overheard his friends saying that they had no intention of being loyal to one company. When I asked why, their stories were similar: their parents sacrificed family time and devoted their lives to their work. Instead of getting the gold watch they were downsized.

It is one of the many examples of how personal history can influence norms. Their generation was affected by an economic downturn, so we can't fault them for being cynical.

A small but diverse company noticed similar attitudes among their new hires and decided to hold weekly lunches devoted to multi-generational sharing. Though there is a new topic each time, the underlying question was the same: "How did your experience shape your perspective?"

Bonding over a common topic made all the difference. The environment has become more respectful and curiosity about each other's viewpoints has everyone willing to engage in conversation.

myth

Knowledge transfer is an impossible challenge

If there isn't a process in place, retiring employees won't be able to pass on essential information, experiences, and know-how.

Institutional wisdom is a valuable commodity that should be treasured. It's important to find a way to access it.

Story

An employee of nearly 40 years become more crabby as he neared retirement. Not knowing what to do with him, they put a plan into place that was so successful they now employ it with every retiree.

The last 4 months of tenure is devoted to sharing institutional wisdom – all those things that long-term employees know that are not written down: lessons learned over the years, customer knowledge, seasonal expectations, and the vast amount of information gained from mere longevity.

Younger staff - many of whom used to make fun of the older employees – hang on their every word, and the veterans are embracing the "young 'uns" for their energy, curiosity, and creative suggestions.

The generation gap has narrowed.

myth

Discussing process during a meeting is a waste of time

A major cause of dysfunction in organizations is miscommunication, most of which stems from focusing on topics, or items, or subject matter rather than on how they're going to be managed, who's going to do what, how related issues are going to be negotiated, or how the problem is going to be solved.

If you find that after getting together, your staff is still discussing how something was mishandled, or they're annoyed with another department, not talking at all, or are complaining about things not getting done on time, then a portion of your meetings should be devoted to process rather than content.

A part of every staff meeting and an occasional retreat should be dedicated to your level of functioning: what's working and what needs improvement.

Story

In an attempt to test this, top management decided to ask two administrative assistants to sit in on meetings and note what topics and information could easily have been distributed through email. The list was endless so they decided to change the weekly meeting's agenda.

A small portion of the time was devoted to clarifying the content, but the bulk of the meeting was focused on process.

myth

The best facilitators are in-house personnel and/or those in charge

They are not the best choice. The decisions made affect them personally and they are bound to have biases which might influence the process. Additionally, any input they offer may be perceived as being biased.

A good facilitator doesn't have a stake in the outcome, only the process. This is what makes it even more frustrating for an internal facilitator who cannot participate because s/he has to remain objective and allied with the entire group.

The best choice is to bring in a contracted professional, or at the least someone from outside the department if you want an internal person.

Story

The Director facilitated a departmental retreat and soon realized that she had two problems. As much as she tried to monitor her body language, her reaction to suggested changes and action steps was so obvious that staff stopped making them. Furthermore, her job was to facilitate so she couldn't share her views.

To the Director's credit, she allowed the last 2 hours to be devoted to talking about her conflict and they all realized that an outside person would be much more beneficial. Though it was a difficult financial and scheduling decision, they decided to reconvene a month later and were relieved to discover that they got much more done.

myth

The size of the group doesn't matter

The larger the group, the smaller the percentage of people who talk, education and status notwithstanding. Too small a group can also be intimidating because the amount of participation expected by each person can be overwhelming.

Story

When the President of a mid-sized company called employees together to make announcements that everyone needed to hear at the same time, everyone listened intently but never asked questions or offered comments.

He decided to ask them to break up into groups of 4 or 5 to generate questions and observations. It's almost impossible not to speak up in a group that size, so almost 100% of the employees contributed.

He also learned the following:
- Hour long meetings were the ideal unless there was a pressing crisis.
- The setting mattered: if meetings were held on the administrative floor, fewer support and production people felt comfortable sharing. If they were on the production floor, the conversation was more inclusive.
- When there was clarity about the purpose of the meeting, it was clear who should be invited, but they were also intent on keeping the group diverse enough to add richness to the discussion.
- When participants understood how their input was valued and used, they were more likely to commit to both the meeting and the discussion.
- And finally, a respectful dialogue ensured a continued dialogue.

myth

There are no benefits to workplace silos

If they didn't have advantages, they wouldn't exist. They're often justified as a way to maintain "departmental pride," and they offer a way to be isolated. Said one staffer "I don't like silos, but everyone leaves us alone and lets us do our work."

Turf protection is a natural tendency, but that doesn't make it right or functional. The lack of information-sharing can seriously affect efficiency, productivity, and good will, and it encourages internal competition, which may waste energy. Further, silos often catch customers in the territorial crossfire and they pick up uncooperative behavior within the organization.

Story

A company was rife with turf wars; there was a sense of pending conflict, which instead of being motivating was uncomfortable and destructive, and customers weren't being well-served.

I met with the department heads. "Too siloed," they said, "too compartmentalized. We don't communicate, we don't share information, we don't feel part of a bigger team."

"I don't believe there aren't some benefits to the silos," I opinioned.

"You don't believe that we hate them?"

"No, I don't believe that at all," I said again.

"But...but they're awful!"

"Well," I said, "The silos have to be doing something for you, or you wouldn't have them," and I suggested they list a few of the benefits - just for kicks.

They were stunned by their list that filled 3 easel pad sheets.

We do what we do because it works for us at some level. In order to change, it's important to acknowledge the trade-offs and make a plan to get the same benefits in a better way.

myth

There's no reason to resist cross-functional training

The one thing we hang on to that makes us feel secure, is the belief that we're necessary and no one else can perform the job as well as we can. The reason many people resist cross-functional training is because they worry that if others are trained to do their jobs, they'll become expendable.

The resistance to cross-training intensifies during times of economic uncertainty when downsizing increases and vulnerability is at its highest.

Story

One company was convinced that if they shared their financial picture with their employees, and held fast to their commitment to retain them and not downsize even during tough times, they would see less resistance to cross-training. It was true.

Seemingly overnight, the workers embraced the cross-training proposal that had been rejected for months. Everyone is now invested in sharing skill-sets and they all have new empathy for each other's challenges.

myth

A good team player is always available

Good team players also need time for themselves - to process information, put ideas together, write reports, and read critical information. Yet asking for alone time is very difficult for most unless it's an agreed-upon priority.

Find a way for people to communicate their need to concentrate and be left alone. If there is a "quiet place" where they can work on something requiring concentration, all the better. If not, a nice sign might suffice.

Story

Everyone was expected to meet deadlines and at the same time always be available to colleagues, so stress levels were off the charts.

They finally set aside a morning to address the problem and learned that all of them, including the administrative assistants, were similarly struggling.

Since there wasn't a private room into which people could go, one of the more creative staff members made up signs that said, "Please interrupt for emergencies only," and personalized each one.

It was so simple, yet it worked. Everyone trusted that when a sign was up, the person really did require privacy. Because the signs also showed the time they would again be available, it turned out that very little fell into the category of emergency.

myth

"We're like a family" is good news

Well, yes and no. When we say, "We're like a family," we usually mean it in a positive way, but most families - even healthy ones - have some level of dysfunction.

Because we're intimately familiar with family dynamics, we often replicate them in the workplace: "You're in my chair; I always sit there during meetings." "They like the A Team better than they like ours." "I think you took that paper that was right here on the corner of my desk." "I don't feel like we should share with the other group." "That was my idea!"

Unfortunately, there's little you can do except be aware of the dynamics and accept some consultation from only children. Since they didn't experience sibling rivalry growing up, they're more likely to look baffled when it's going on at work, and less likely to react to it.

Story

Whenever someone says we're a family, the staff of a large non-profit responds, "No, we want to be functional!" I remember an old cartoon showing a sign announcing a "Conference For Functional Families" and only two people were in the audience.

Families, like teams who work closely with one another, sometimes find it helpful to operate under the philosophy, "We are a complicated group, but we love each other anyway."

Look at your personal relationships and learn from them. My husband and I have been married for about 1000 years. He's one of 3 and I'm an only child. To this day, if we're cutting cake, he looks to see how big my piece is.

One day I asked him why. "I don't know," he said "I can't stop," and we laughed about it. I hope that people find it just as funny in the workplace, while being cognizant of how it may affect the environment.

myth

Workplace Culture

myth

Company Mission and Vision Statements are an integral part of employee awareness

Beautiful plaques engraved with Mission and Vision Statements hang on the walls for all to see and sometimes the statements appear on the backs of business cards carried by employees wherever they go. But if you stop those same employees in the hall, they probably couldn't recite either statement, or wouldn't understand their meaning, or wouldn't have any idea how the statements are manifest in their company's day-to-day activities.

Story

A large company hired expensive consultants to help further refine the Mission and Vision statements and to design a beautiful logo.

After the consultants left, an employee observed "Now we have beautifully articulated mission and vision statements, and even a pretty logo to go long with them, but it still doesn't help because we don't practice what we profess to believe!"

The crafting of the mission and vision statements is rarely the issue, but integrating them throughout the company culture is another story.

Management (with employee consultation) committed to reviewing all their practices and procedures to assure conformance with their professed philosophy and to do whatever they could to help their employees be more in alignment.

At first it took constant reminding. After a while, it became the norm. New hires were appraised of the culture and if there wasn't a fit, they weren't offered positions regardless of their talent and expertise.

myth

We consistently practice what we preach

Symbolism is very powerful. There are probably a lot of little practices that don't reflect the company values such as club memberships for select people, special parking spots, inequitable lunch breaks, larger offices awarded for status, closed door conversations, or hidden pay scales.

To test this out in your organization, give everyone your mission, vision, and values statements and ask them to list anything the company does that counters the message. In other words, ask them if your organization practices what it preaches and see how close you come.

Story

A well-meaning CEO stated, both in writing and verbally, that their workplace was one of equality, that status was less important than equity, and that everyone was treated the same. He, however, had numerous perks not available to anyone else: only company officers were on the top floor, his office was huge and surrounded by windows, and if an all staff meeting was scheduled that he couldn't attend, it was canceled.

As well meaning as he was, there was a disconnect between what he said he believed and the many small ways employees were reminded of who was more important.

Another CEO was rightly proud of his self-directed, equitable environment. One day I said to him, "I notice that you still have a designated parking place by the front door. No matter how much you tell people they're equal and as essential as you, that parking place delivers a very different message about who is really the most important person in the company."

He now gets to park there only if he arrives first in the morning.

myth

An egalitarian environment
leads to an undermining of authority

On the contrary, when there is equality, people know they will be heard, that their influence will be welcomed, and that they don't have a need to rebel against authority. Further, if the environment isn't to their liking they have permission to try making changes.

Look at societal upheaval. It isn't people with power who rebel, it's those for whom life is inequitable. Whether it's riots by small disenfranchised groups or by thousands of people who have been kept down by a regime, rebellion emerges from inequality. In addition to dramatic reactions, there can also be quiet but steady push back.

Story

An Executive Director prided himself on being decisive which, for his employees, translated into him being dictatorial. He shouted orders and made it clear that his expectations were the only ones that counted.

Little by little, staff members began undermining his authority because it was the only way they felt they could have an impact. The organization ended up going through massive upheaval that could easily have been avoided.

The Board of Directors felt that their mission and vision were being compromised and held him accountable for the near demise of the non-profit because his self-proclaimed elevated status disenfranchised and marginalized everyone else.

Sadly, none of the staff advocated for him.

myth

Employees will feel included if you just ask them for input

Leaders understand that employee input can provide needed expertise and excellent information and insights that may well be essential to running the organization, so they often ask for it, but with mixed results.

It takes more than just asking. If you want employees engaged and willing to continue sharing opinions, you need to respond to their ideas and suggestions.

Employees want their say but they don't necessarily need their way. They'll understand if all their suggestions can't be used, but they will not tolerate being ignored!

You need to thank them for responding, and tell them the reasons that some suggestions are being implemented and some aren't. They're fine with not getting all they want, but they are not fine when there is no explanation. If you don't communicate with them in a timely manner, there's a good chance they won't be responsive in the future.

Story

The Executive Team wondered what they were doing wrong. They continually sought suggestions from employees but got nowhere, so I asked what happened the first time they encouraged employees to share opinions.

They distributed a survey focused on strategic approaches and new products. Everyone really got into it and provided excellent feedback. Management read and seriously considered every single response but then realized they couldn't implement most of the suggestions because their finances had abruptly changed.

No one explained to the employees why their ideas couldn't be used, so they thought their feedback was not even read and that the entire exercise was a waste of effort. From then on, they no longer bothered to respond.

myth

Everyone does not need to know the "total picture"

Employees may not need to know, but they probably want to know so that their jobs have meaning. Their motivation is increased when, instead of feeling like a mere cog in a wheel, they know the wheel won't work without them.

Story

A company was making a small part for a machine that helped medical professionals assess the status of their patients' health. Productivity was low because people worked slowly and without enthusiasm, so the supervisor brought in a video of patients describing how early detection had prevented a serious illness.

Productivity shot up and remained at high levels. Employees realized that their efforts were essential and their contributions valuable. What previously seemed like a boring process manufacturing an insignificant machine part was now tied to a very important mission.

myth

Celebrations should be held
only after a project is completed

By the time a project is completed in a fast-paced organization, employees are on to the next one and there's often no time to celebrate. Acknowledgment of a job well done does not have to be reserved for the end. Why not enjoy milestones and take a few minutes to congratulate those who have completed their part?

Story

An architectural/engineering firm recognized that they never celebrated anything because there were always looming deadlines. They also noticed that any kudos given out were received by managers and not shared with the numerous employees who made the projects a success.

Now they have "milestone celebrations" that occur along the way and recognize all those who made the next steps possible. It doesn't take much: pizza, pastries, going out to lunch, or a mention in the company newsletter.

Motivation and morale have increased and employees are much more appreciative of each other's contributions.

myth

People should leave their personal problems at the door

Exactly where are people supposed to leave them? In a receptacle in the front lobby? Is it big enough to hold everyone's problems? Aren't people worried that they'll take the wrong ones home at the end of the day? "I came to work with a problem, but you should see the doozie I went home with!"

Though it might be an attractive option, it is not possible to leave anything "at the door."

We're finally realizing that if employees can safely say "I'm going through a hard time," or "I've had a difficult weekend," or "I have an ill family member," they can get on with their work. If they have to keep it to themselves, that's where their energy goes and they'll probably be less productive.

Story

Many larger companies have seen the light and have in-house psychologists or access the services of an Employee Assistance Program.

EAPs are intended to help employees deal with personal problems that might adversely affect their work performance, health, and general well-being. EAPs can include assessment, short-term counseling, and referral services for both the employees and their household members. Some even provide coaching for supervisors.

These services are not being offered just because it's the kind and right thing to do. It also makes economic sense. It's far more cost-effective to help a well-trained employee through a difficult time than it is to hire a new one and it delivers the message that you care.

myth

Customer complaints are almost always an indicator of employee error

There is always another side to any story. It's critical that you get input from the employee who dealt with the customer, not in an angry or accusatory manner, but by engaging in a simple, respectful conversation. This will go a long way to deliver the message that "our staff is as important as the people we serve."

If employees are not accused, they won't be defensive, so try beginning conversations by saying, "This is what we heard from the customer. What do you think?" If it's simply an inquiry, the explanation will be forthcoming.

Once the situation is understood, consider having the employee help create or even deliver the response to the customer by signing the letter or making the call.

Story

A customer called the Executive Director saying that she had requested information but felt ignored because no one ever got back to her.

The ED was furious because it was the second time that week that he'd heard a similar complaint. He flew out into the hall and berated both the Program Director and her administrative assistant.

Turns out that in both cases, a glitch in their IT system sent the inquiring emails to spam. Had the ED handled it appropriately, the staff members would have felt respected and the customer would have had a proper explanation.

myth

The Customer is always right

Customers are not always right. They're often wrong, misinformed, lacking in understanding, or off the mark. Of course the customer deserves respect – as does everyone – but they're not always right.

Story

A frustrated group of call center employees had had it! The company's motto was "The customer is always right" which meant that employees had to either give customers what they wanted or take their abuse because disagreeing with them in any way was considered bad business.

Eventually, a new CEO came in and had the good sense to listen to the team and ask for their suggestions.

Now they empathize with the customers and tell them they will do everything in their power to help. However, they are also free to say, "Perhaps there has been a misunderstanding. Here is how we see it. How does that differ from your perspective?" They don't take the blame if it's undeserved but they're happy to take responsibility for helping to rectify the problem.

myth

"Customer First" is the best policy

Perhaps this long-standing customer service mantra should be changed to "Employee First!" Happy employees result in happy customers. When the waitress smiles, my experience is nicer. When the salesperson is pleasant, I want to buy more. If energy is directed to ensuring that employees are happy and respected, it spills over to customers and moves businesses forward.

In organizations where they hire right, train people well, celebrate successes, and involve their employees in decisions that affect them, people have the energy to deal with the unanticipated issues of the day. They're pleasant because they're revered. Who doesn't work well in such a respectful environment? That satisfaction spills over to their interactions with customers or clients.

Story

Taking a collective deep breath, the Executives declared that, from now on, it was going to be an "Employee Centered" environment. They would do everything within their financial ability to make sure that those who worked with them were satisfied, well-served, and supported. Their benefits would be at the top of the scale that they could afford, and if they weren't good enough, the employees would be told the reason.

Veteran employees were a bit suspicious because it was so unusual and different from how they had operated. When they hit the 8-month mark, it became clear that the new value was permanent. Even they had not realized the results until customers started commenting on how wonderful it was to deal with them.

The energy they previously used defending their actions was now used to service their clients.

myth

If we adopt a blame-free organization no one will be accountable

Quite the opposite is true. Taking responsibility for mistakes is much easier if the environment isn't punitive. In a blame-free organization, accountability increases because it's safer.

It doesn't matter who is to blame. What does matter is that what's not working gets fixed. The employees who have the information and are able to help are the ones who "do the fixing" by talking with one another rather than following the parent/child model of reporting to their supervisors who then report to other supervisors.

Story

A forward-thinking CEO agreed to try a blame-free environment.

He knew it was a dramatic change for his company and that it would take about a year to make the transition, so he established a procedure that reminded everyone that when something wasn't working, they had to involve those with information that could help, and that they should always communicate respectively and effectively.

The most exciting result was that most everyone is now willing to come forward and say, "I made a mistake" or "I blew it" or "I'm sorry that I failed."

In a blame-free environment it's much easier to take responsibility because it's solution-oriented and doesn't put people on the defensive.

Their remaining challenge is not blaming others for blaming!

myth

Gossip is inevitable

Not if you decide to have a gossip-free environment.

It's an easy concept to understand and a hard one to implement, but it's possible. The gossip-free environment is one where we talk to people instead of about people.

If someone complains to you about a colleague, you don't stop them by telling them they're gossiping; instead you ask "How can I help you find the best way to speak with that person directly?"

Story

It takes at least a year to achieve a gossip-free environment, and this one organization proudly announced it had finally reached that goal, so I asked an employee what it was like to work there. "It's the most boring but safest place on earth," he said.

Sure, they missed talking about people around the coffee pot, but they did not miss being the subject of those discussions one bit! And because they worked out their issues with one another, if colleagues smiled at them, they knew the gesture was sincere.

When asked to describe their work environment, employees said: relaxed, safe, happy, and secure.

(A few years ago I heard that an anthropologist was trying to figure out how language developed. Among his conclusions he suggested that there may have been a need to gossip, so I pictured this guy standing in front of a cave thinking, "I hate that guy and I have no words.")

myth

Rumors are a result of nosey employees wanting to start trouble

To the extent there are rumors is the extent to which people don't have information, and when they can't get it they often become anxious, frustrated, or even angry.

Further, because the unknown is unnerving, people tend to make up stories which may be even worse, so even if you have nothing to share, tell them so they know you're not keeping anything from them.

You can be upset with rumors or you can view them as the barometer that tells you when your employees need to hear from you.

Story

A few years ago, I was on a plane that was still on the tarmac 20 minutes after its scheduled takeoff. The passengers began getting edgy, wondering whether they'd make their connections, and couldn't help but make up stories about the reason behind the delay.

Finally the pilot spoke up: "You're all going to make your connections, but you deserve to know why we're not taking off. Apparently the machine that smashes your luggage has broken so we have to do it by hand!"

Crabby as he was, the guy next to me started laughing. The pilot had diffused the tension by making a connection with the passengers, even though it wasn't all that helpful. He let us know that we hadn't been forgotten.

myth

Employees who still have their jobs during difficult economic times will be even more supportive of one another

When times are tough and the pie is smaller, even people who are working become concerned about job security and start protecting their own turf and excluding others.

When things get tight, increased prejudice and discrimination are more likely to emerge, and it's more tempting to marginalize work-mates to ensure that "there's more for me."

Story

Over the years, a manufacturing plant became more diverse and lead-ership took pride in their inclusiveness, often pointing out that there was little or no discrimination.

Then tough times hit. Almost overnight, ethnic, racial, and gender-related slurs infiltrated the workplace. When employees were remind-ed that this behavior would not be tolerated, the rhetoric stopped, but exclusion did not. Even after a few people were let go for their inappropriate behavior, separateness hung in the air.

Then they secured a huge contract that assured everyone's security for a number of years. They had a company-wide cookout to celebrate. People seemed more relaxed and the ice began to melt. As the months went by, it felt like they were going back to the days of acceptance and inclusion.

Instead of simply enjoying the lack of tension, the HR Director put the episode on the agenda for periodic meetings so they could all discuss what had happened and what they could do to ensure that it wouldn't happen again, regardless of outside forces.

myth

An efficiently run workplace
needs tightly controlled break times

Everyone has their own work habits and knows what they need to function.

Just because people are at their stations doesn't mean they're working efficiently. Some have back issues and need to take frequent, short walks. Some need lots of coffee to keep them going. Some have small bladders and need more bathroom breaks, some may be hypoglycemic and need frequent food breaks to keep their blood sugar constant, and some may need to regroup after a stressful project deadline is met.

Adults know when they need a break, so let them decide.

Story

For years the agency had very strict rules about break and lunch times. 10:00-10:15 was the morning break. Lunch was segmented between 11:30 and 1:00, and the afternoon break was at 3. If someone was busy during the allotted times, they missed out.

So people found ways to get around it. They fibbed about when they left or came back, staged fictional appointments, and refused to work through any portion of lunch or break times regardless of demands.

When the new boss arrived, he decided that such rigidity was not only unnecessary but insulting to a staff who had long ago proven its worth. He did away with the strict scheduling and asked employees to be responsible.

A few took advantage at the beginning, but their colleagues called them on it and now when someone takes a break, nobody blinks. They trust each other and assume the person is in need and will be back on time.

The culture, not the rules, demands responsibility.

myth

Time clocks don't hurt morale

There may be some work environments where time clocks are part of the culture and where most employees don't question their use, but in many workplace situations, they are an insult and can interfere with the process of building trust.

Story

2 employees took unfair advantage of break times at a small manufacturing plant that had been in business for 40 years, so management decided to install a time clock.

The reaction was swift and dramatic. People were furious and hurt. "I've worked here 25 years and have never been late or left early unless it was an emergency. How dare they not trust me?"

People started cheating the system: they had others punch in or out for them, they'd take longer breaks than usual, and they slacked off while on the job.

Distrust leads to distrustful behavior.

myth

It's important to keep salaries secret

The National Labor Relations Act says that employers cannot prevent employees from discussing wages and working conditions among themselves.

Legal or not, I can't think of any reason to be secretive unless there are inequities in how people are being reimbursed and the decision-makers are embarrassed about their policies.

Story

I once asked a CEO why he didn't disclose salaries. He was as surprised by the question as I was by the policy. I took advantage of his baffled silence to ask him if he paid industry standard.

"Higher!" he replied, so I asked why he wasn't proud of that and why he didn't want to shout it from the rooftops!

It turns out that many of his employees wondered whether they were being underpaid and whether people with similar jobs at other companies were making more.

With some trepidation, he posted salary ranges. He was shocked by the enormous interest and the employees were surprised by the equitable salaries. The only criticism that could be heard was, "I wonder why they didn't tell us this a long time ago. It turns out that there was nothing to hide."

myth

Economics and logistics should be the major focus when considering Mergers and Acquisitions

A major reason for the high failure rate of M&A's is due to a lack of cultural integration because the "people" aspect is often the last to be addressed.

Those planning the merger or acquisition focus on product, geography, and money. By the time they think about the workplace environment, the stress and tension among the employees may be beyond resolution.

Story

Because two organizations shared the same product, mission, and vision, merging seemed like an easy decision, even though one company was hierarchical and the other self-directed. After attending to production, market share, location, and finances, the leadership team decided that it was the perfect marriage, so they merged.

It was a disaster.

After a few months the administrators decided to bring together employees from the two organizations. The group was clearly divided with an imaginary but all too real line down the middle of the room.

After HR struggled to get a conversation started, one woman finally raised her hand and said, "This is like IBM merging with Ben and Jerry's! Who would do that?"

For the very first time since the merger, people laughed.

Had HR worked with the employees to develop a new culture, it wouldn't have taken nearly a year to salvage the merger, and they would not have lost so many talented people because the process started so late.

Final Thoughts

myth

Taking pride in the success of your employees is enough

If you're going to take pride in your employees' successes, you have to take some responsibility for their failures.

Story

When all was going well the sales director puffed up and talked about how proud he was when sales reached higher than anticipated levels. There was always a celebratory cake on Friday afternoons. After all, acknowledging success is a good thing!

However if sales were down or mistakes were made, his first response was "Who's at fault?" His energy went into finding out what went wrong, chastising others, and insisting that it shouldn't happen again.

Rarely did he ask what systemic issues might have played a part: was it lack of training, poor processes, or inflated projections? Or maybe it was a misunderstanding of customer needs and/or process confusion? He never explored what role he might have played in the outcome.

Finally a frustrated colleague said, "Make up your mind. Selective responsibility is not working."

He was understandably shaken by the critique, but to his credit, he took it to heart and began sharing responsibility (which is different from blame) for the negative as well as the positive.

myth

The main criteria
for an effective Board of Directors/Advisors
is to care about the mission

That's a start, but it does not necessarily result in a coalesced group. Like every other team, a Board has to evolve and its members will function much more effectively if they have a keen understanding of each other's styles and areas of expertise.

Story

A wonderful and well-known organization dedicated itself to advocating for the disadvantaged. Everyone they recruited for their Board had a passion for the people they served and a history of focusing on their needs. But year after year, they struggled with conflict, differing visions, and divergent styles that threatened their effectiveness and even their existence.

Though they had yearly retreats to engage in strategic planning, they had never allotted time for assessing their own functioning. They finally admitted that time wasn't the issue. They were just afraid to engage in personal conversations and weren't sure how to handle what might come up.

They decided to take the leap and spend two full days on self-assessment. After articulating the issues, they shared their individual approaches, communication styles, and hopes. It was painful, agonizing, sometimes fun, and always illuminating.

They soon learned that most of their tension was a result of stylistic differences rather than incompatible goals. They spent the second day reconfiguring their meetings and coming up with a process that worked for all, while committing to conflict resolution as a high priority.

myth

We don't have time to deal with this stuff

Whenever you say, "We don't have time," ask yourself, "Do I have time not to? Because if I don't address it now, how much time is it likely to take later on?"

Responding to and dealing with problems sooner than later saves time down the road and is more likely to preserve relationships.

Story

The COO's most common statement was, "I don't have time for this." A trusted colleague pointed out that he said this only when he wanted to avoid certain difficult issues and problems, so he vowed to work on it.

Instead of his usual rhetoric, he simply began saying, "I'm choosing not to take the time to deal with it."

Little by little, he tread into areas that he would rather have avoided. It became incrementally easier, so much so that he shared his experience with the rest of the leadership team.

Now everyone recognizes it's okay to say "I'm not going to take the time now," but they're committed to making sure they take it later.

myth

You have to listen to people like me

No, you don't.

Story

It's YOURS and it's your professional life.

As I said in the introduction, take what makes sense, throw out what doesn't, and put on the shelf what you want to take down some day.

Made in the USA
Middletown, DE
01 August 2015